T0285320

DOG & GOD

The Coincidences of Collective Unconscious

DR. HELEN SEVIC

DOG and GOD

The Coincidences of Collective Unconscious

Print ISBN: 979-8-35096-916-0
eBook ISBN: 979-8-35096-917-7

CONTENTS

Preface 1

1. Introduction 4

2. Words from Heaven 13

3. The Roots of Alphabets 25

4. Scientific Symbols 41

5. The Color of Life 61

6. The Pareidolia Rocks 85

7. The Pareidolia Earth 100

8. The Unconscious Map 129

9. Making Unconscious Mind Conscious 147

About the Author 155

"In this collective unconscious, we are all linked together, like islands in the sea. We may appear to be separate on the surface, but deep down, at the roots of our being, we are united."

—CARL JUNG

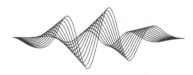

"Imagination is more important than knowledge. Knowledge is limited. Imagination encircles the world."

—ALBERT EINSTEIN

PREFACE

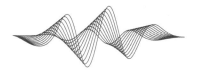

My husband often jokes that I am a pattern recognition machine, always spotting patterns in everyday life that he cannot see. This trait has been with me since childhood. In class, when I was bored, I would doodle imaginative scenes, like a human growing as a tree, with feet as roots, hands as flowers, and the head as the fruit. When I felt down, I'd draw twisted human trees. As I grew, I naturally saw trees and plants that resembled human forms. My phone is now filled with pictures of nature mimicking human faces. This phenomenon, known as pareidolia, is a psychological tendency more common in childhood but has stayed with me.

This gift benefited me during my first job application when IBM China selected fresh graduates with English and IQ tests. While we all struggled with the foreign language, I excelled in the IQ test, which relied heavily on recognizing patterns—a natural skill for me.

In today's job market, companies may prioritize solid skills over instinctual pattern recognition. Yet, pattern recognition has always been a cornerstone of scientific inquiry and philosophical reflection. These patterns help us understand the universe and humanity by unveiling the principles that govern natural phenomena. Mathematics and physics are built on pattern abstraction, leading to significant discoveries and inventions. I am particularly fascinated by fractal simulation, which began with the self-similar patterns of plants and snowflakes and evolved to simulate coastlines, mountains, and even fire accurately. It is my belief that soon in future we will be able to simulate our thoughts after we understand the core patterns that govern our conscious.

During my university studies in vibration analysis, I learned about natural frequency and resonance. I realized that not only mechanical systems but also the human body have modes of vibration that cause resonant responses. This concept of resonance helps me understand social phenomena, such as the power of prayer and the impact of historical geniuses. My experience in personality analysis has strengthened my belief that life follows certain patterns. The more we recognize these patterns, the less confusing life becomes. Modern societal trends, like the rise of homosexuality, gender transformation, and the lost reproductive drives, seem strange only when misunderstood. Through the lens of Yin-Yang philosophy, when we can see the universal reversal patterns of lifecycles, these phenomena will become completely understandable.

I used to think my 11 years of higher education at Tsinghua University were wasted since I did not become an engineer. However, my education empowered me with logical thinking, preventing me from blindly believing in things I don't understand. Combining my instinct for pattern recognition with logical reasoning led me to the comprehension of Carl Jung's concept of the collective unconscious and his complex book, "Synchronicity: An Acausal Connecting Principle," which explores meaningful coincidences connected by meaning rather than causality. From my experiences, these coincidences can be explained and understood by understanding of collective unconscious and archetype, the common patterns underneath that govern our conscious minds. Most coincidences in life should not be ignored, as they contain deep meanings and serve as life's messengers.

Although my original motivation for writing this book was my passion, I believe it will appeal to readers who enjoy understanding the mysteries of the world rationally and appreciate bold, new ideas. I hope this book helps those who feel stuck between belief and reason to find a way out, gain confidence in humanity's future, and feel fortunate to be human.

I would like to thank my family, who has always unconditionally supported my all-consuming and aimless hobby. My father, who would remind me to "take my medicine" when he saw me overexcited with strange ideas to his traditional mind, and my mother, who watches my incomprehensible drawings even though she enjoys more if I paint birds and flowers with her. My daughter, who, on her 10th birthday, asked me to change my book's title to "DOG & GOD" as a special birthday gift for her. Her love and appreciation for my writing motivate me to publish this book.

Thanks to my husband, who, despite his scientific genes, has been nothing but positive and supportive with full ears to my "nonsenses". Had he not given me rational encouragement with two great books, Goethe's "The Theory of Colors" and Schrodinger's "What is Life," my "GOD & DOG" might never have become a reality.

Thanks to my friend and coworker Tang Gefeng, who guided me when I was perplexed and introduced me to Jung's works. They have become a lighthouse in my quest for understanding, illuminating the darkness of the unknown.

CHAPTER 1

INTRODUCTION

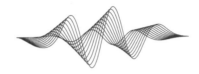

1.1 The Artifact of Nonsense

The English word "nonsense" combines "sense" with the prefix "non-," literally meaning "not sensed." However, its actual meaning is "ridiculous" or "absurd." This reflects the common notion that things which cannot be sensed do not make sense. In fact, things we cannot sense are not all nonsense. For example, humans can perceive only a small portion of the physical universe. Just as visible light represents only a tiny segment of the electromagnetic spectrum, we cannot see phenomena like microwaves, X-rays, and radio waves without objective proof of their existence.

> "Man has developed consciousness slowly and laboriously,
> in a process that took untold ages to reach the civilized
> state. And this evolution is far from complete, for large areas
> of the human mind are still shrouded in darkness."
>
> —CARL JUNG

The aim of this book is to awaken a dark world to common sense, the collective unconscious as defined by Carl Jung over a century ago. I believe that the collective unconscious contains many things, and making its contents conscious will lead to a significant expansion of our understanding and knowledge.

In our society, the concepts of true and false are often dictated by the majority's views. What the "normal majority" believes becomes accepted as true. Blind people do not argue that darkness is the true nature of the world, and the colorblind do not claim the limited spectrum represents the entirety of reality. They trust the majority's judgment that what they sense is abnormal and thus not reality. But is this perceived "normal" reality? After all, the vibrant colors we see are merely artifacts created by our eyes interpreting light absorbed and reflected from various surfaces.

In reality, there is no common worldview held even by the normal majority. Instead, different perceptions lead to endless conflicts among individuals, families, political parties, and nations. As knowledge grows, these divergent perceptions become even more pronounced, increasing division of parties. This highlights a simple fact that is easy to agree with but often forgotten:

The essence of the world is a series of different perceptions. It may not be a coincidence that the Chinese word for "world" (世界, shìjiè) sounds identical to the word for "perception" (视界, shìjiè), revealing the truth "世界=视界 (the world equals to perception)."

Most of the ideas in my book may sound like complete nonsense to those who only believe in proven knowledge or common sense. When I come up with ideas that go beyond common perceptions, I also question the value of these unconventional thoughts that always excite me. At these moments, an old fable often comes to mind: the story of the blind men who each touch a different part of an elephant and guess what it looks like. The one who touches the elephant's back thinks it resembles a wall, while the one who touches the tail thinks it resembles a rope.

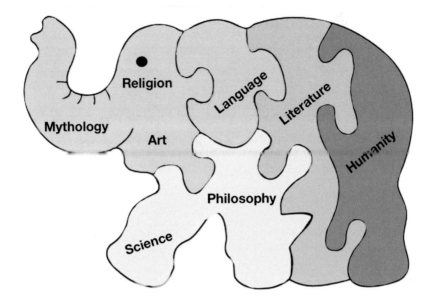

This fable mirrors our society, where domain knowledge becomes increasingly specialized. Even if someone dedicated their entire life to studying, they would only scratch the tip of the iceberg of human knowledge. If you cannot comprehend that others' different perceptions may also be valid or that what lies beyond your senses may exist, then you are no different from the blind man who judges an elephant by only touching its tail.

Picturing this elephant makes me think that the limitations and entrenched errors of human cognition stem from our inability to overcome our blind spots. These missing truths and fallacies are not hidden far beyond our sight; rather, they are concealed in plain view, covered by judgment, and dismissed as nonsense.

Unlike conventional schools of thought, this book focuses on coincidences within the collective unconscious that are often ignored or deemed nonsensical. I hope to bring these overlooked puzzle pieces from the depths of the collective unconscious to the surface, continuing the mission started by the great pioneers. As Carl Jung said, "Man's task is to become conscious of the contents that press upward from the unconscious."

1.2 Collective Unconscious and Archetypes

Often there comes a time in one's life, usually in their 50s or so, that they will look back upon the branching decision tree that shaped their life here-to-now, and realize that many of these decisions were not of their own design, but rather arrangements of "fate". "Fate" denotes the unsensed forces that shape our lives and are often unconscious. It exerts an omnipresent control over our lives. As Carl Jung said, "Until you make the unconscious conscious, it will direct your life and you will call it fate."

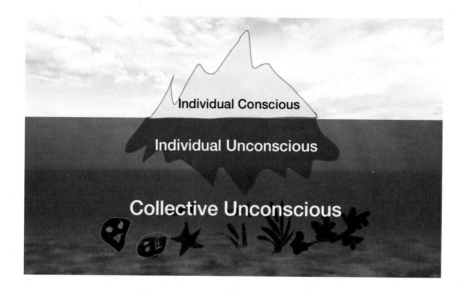

Freud divided the mind into three psychological forces: the conscious, the subconscious, and the unconscious. He used the analogy of an iceberg to describe his model. He believed the conscious to be the tip of the iceberg: the small part of mental activity that we are aware of, whereas the unconscious is like the submerged portion of the iceberg: unseen yet constituting the bulk of one's mental activity. He took the subconscious to be the vastly more powerful internal forces behind human behavior. From this foundation, his student Carl Jung further distinguished between two levels of the unconscious: the personal unconscious and the collective unconscious, as he defined below:

"In addition to our immediate consciousness, which is of a thoroughly personal nature and which we believe to be the only empirical psyche (even if we tack on the personal unconscious as an appendix), there exists a second psychic system of a collective, universal, and impersonal nature which is identical in all individuals. This collective unconscious does not develop individually but is inherited. It consists of pre-existent forms, the archetypes, which can only become conscious secondarily and which give definite form to certain psychic contents."

–CARL JUNG

By understanding Jung's distinction between the personal and collective unconscious, we gain insight into how deeply interconnected and influenced we are by universal patterns and symbols that transcend personal experience. The concept of archetypes is the key to understand the universal patterns as a key feature of collective unconscious.

"Archetypes are typical modes of apprehension, and wherever we meet with uniform and regularly recurring modes of apprehension, we are dealing with an archetype, no matter whether its mythological character is recognized or not."

–CARL JUNG

Carl Jung's concept of archetypes refers to the idea that there are universal, primordial images and themes that reside in the collective unconscious, shared by all humans. These archetypes are inherited rather than learned and appear in various cultural narratives and symbols. They can be found in myths, fairy tales, religious stories, and modern storytelling. Examples of archetypes given by Carl Jung include:

- **The Self**: The unification of the conscious and unconscious.

- **The Shadow**: The unknown, dark side of the personality.

- **The Anima/Animus**: The feminine aspect in men and the masculine aspect in women.

- **The Hero**: Represents the struggle and eventual triumph over adversity.

- **The Mother**: Symbolizes nurturing and caretaking.

While Carl Jung focused his concepts of the collective unconscious and archetypes within the dedicated domain of psychology to understand human psyche and behavior, my application of these concepts has broader views and more profound significance. Through my books, I aim to demonstrate that the collective unconscious and archetypes provide the best explanations for the phenomena of meaningful coincidences that often elude our normal perception. This understanding allows us to grasp the true meanings of the greatest mythologies and religions, not just through pure belief but with reason. Ultimately, this approach bridges the gap between science and religion, a division that has long hindered our ability to break through the blind spots in our perception. As Einstein aptly said, "Science without religion is lame, religion without science is blind."

1.3 Phenomena of Coincidences

No doubt, throughout your life you have encountered many fascinating coincidences. The normal consciousness perceives coincidences to be meaningless random events, so they are not taken seriously. However, when I consciously inspected the vast collection of life's various coincidences, I discovered that coincidences are not random, rather they occur in collective and continuous patterns undergirded by certain common principles.

This book presents a collection of coincidences I have observed over the last 20 years. These include patterns in word structures and formations, colors in flags and logos, and recurring themes in maps and satellite images that reflect regional history, culture, legends, and mythologies.

The title of the book "Dog & God" represents a coincidence of word formation: if the order of the letters in DOG are reversed, it becomes

GOD. Similarly, "live" flipped around becomes "evil" and the letter M, standing for "Mountain" and "Man," when flipped around becomes the letter W, which stands for "Water" and "Woman". Before our eyes, word structures and alphabetic sequences give rise to universal rules and patterns within the circle of life.

Following these patterns, I found many words that share this reversal pattern. "Evolve," consisting of three pairs and six letters, displays the same universal rule of life defined by the Chinese "Book of Changes" (*Yi Jing*): from start to finish, all things evolve through three stages and six processes. Moreover, the beginning (ev) and the ending (ve) are reversed, as the beginning and end of the name of Eve. The central characters of "evolve", "ol = 01", become "lo=10" after reversal showing that life is not simply repetition, but rather spirals forward in a helix-like evolutionary pattern.

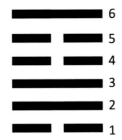

The letter structure of "evolve" holds more meaning yet: the foremost and last letter, "e", originates from the Egyptian hieroglyph of a human figure (𓀀). The hieroglyph of this "person" is barren of detail and lush with meaning. Its hands raise upward, the feet point backwards to the left, whereas the body is sketched with lines pointing up and to the right, implying the direction of human evolution runs from left to right, from bottom to the top, but in the end we will turn around and head from the top down to our ancestral roots. Of the 26 letters of the Roman alphabet, "e" is the only archetype of a human figure and happen to be the most frequently used letter within human writing systems.

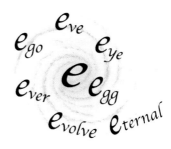

The lowercase letter "e" looks like a curly fetus or a spiral galaxy. "e" is also the scientific symbol for electrons and the electronic world. Although the original meaning of "human" is lost to history, the essence of "e" is alive in the collective unconscious, leading many words related to human origin including eve, egg, eye, ego, earth, evolve, eternal, etc.

These "nonsense" coincidences intrigue me. For over 20 years, collecting coincidences has become an obsession. The process of observing, collecting, thinking, and imagining these coincidences is like playing a puzzle, putting together pieces from a pile of chaos into a coherent whole of clear order and logic. Jung's theories have allowed me to transform this aimless hobby into a discovery of the mysteries lurking within the seabed of collective unconsciousness. I believe coincidences are neither random nor meaningless. They are important messengers connecting our conscious minds with the largely unknown realm of the collective unconscious.

Since the unconscious mind, particularly the deeper collective unconscious, lies far beyond our normal conscious awareness, it is not natural to make the unconscious mind conscious. It took me a long time to understand why and how I can easily perceive the meanings of many coincidences while others cannot or find it very difficult. I have summarized the insights I gained from my experiences in the last chapter (Chapter 9). I did this because I prefer not to influence others directly and hope the presence of these coincidences will inspire and surprise them as they did to me. However, if you find it difficult to read the book or think the ideas are non-sensical, you can check my rationales presented in Chapter 9: Making the Unconscious Mind Conscious.

Now, read the following quotes and prepare yourself for a journey of discovery into the unknown world.

"In all chaos, there is a universe and a secret order; among all phenomena, there is a unified law...What we call complexity and miracles is not complicated and magical at all in nature, on the contrary, it is simple and common. We are used to project our own difficulties in understanding to things and to describe them as complex, but in fact, they are very simple and do not understand the difficulties we encounter intellectually."

–CARL JUNG

"The desire of knowledge is first stimulated in us when remarkable phenomena attract our attention. In order that this attention be continued, it is necessary that we should feel some interest in exercising it. And thus by degrees we become better acquainted with the object of our curiosity. During this process of observation we remark at first only a vast variety which presses indiscriminately on our view; we are forced to separate, to distinguish, and again to combine; by which means, at last a certain order arises which admits of being surveyed with more or less satisfaction"

–GOETHE'S THEORY OF COLORS: WITH NOTES 1840

CHAPTER 2

WORDS FROM HEAVEN

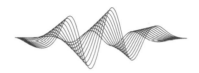

The saying goes that a picture is worth a thousand words. Yet, we often overlook that a single word itself is a scroll of pictures, manifesting a record of history. Each word is a divine picture and a book from heaven.

Starting with the letter structures in "DOG" and "GOD," I have discovered countless coincidences among letters and phonetics. This has led me to realize that words are not merely man-made communication tools but rather an organic system—a visible garment covering the invisible soul of humanity. Words are intertwined with human civilization, creating an archaeological record from its origins to the present. They originate from archetypes engraved in the collective human unconscious.

The following examples demonstrate how words carry meanings beyond individual consciousness and have evolved in parallel with the historical journey of humanity.

2.1 Book of Philosophy

To the Western eye, Chinese characters look more like drawings. Truly, if you carefully examine the structure of each Chinese character, you will find them to be not a simple drawing, but a series of illustrations making up a continuous philosophical scroll.

On the left of the chart you will find the simplest word "人", meaning "person", which is composed of two strokes leaning on each other. This indicates that at its core, a "per-

son" is the unity of two sexes, the product of the genes of the paternal and maternal lineages coming together. It could also be seen as a pair of legs, representing the "split" nature of humanity.

The middle character, "个", meaning "individual", retains the split of "person" but with a central pillar, implying that to be an independent individual, one needs to support their two independent sides. The left-right split from its original "人" doesn't disappear but is pushed up to a more cerebral position at its head.

The rightmost character on the chart, "众", meaning "masses", depicts a social nature. In it, three "persons" are piled up, with one standing up on the shoulders of the two others. The egotistic central pillars of "individual" persons are removed. It illustrates vividly the nature of a group society: It is a hierarchical structure. In order to get along as a social group, one has to sacrifice some individual personality, e.g. the central pillar of individual, and support the leader on top.

Together, these three simple words illustrate a concise philosophical distinction between the individual and social attributes of human nature. The ancestors who first devised these characters likely did not consciously communicate their meaning in this way. Instead, it was the universal archetype of the collective unconscious that guided the instincts of individual consciousness to embody these characters as they are.

The two following examples show how the structural changes in historical words synchronize with the changes in the social value system at the time.

First, let's look at the evolution of a well-known word, "道", which is the "Tao" in western spelling, the oldest Chinese philosophy of nature's law.

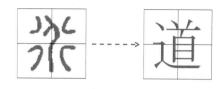

The structure of the original bronze inscriptions of Tao, shown to the left on above diagram, contains a bent human body surrounded in all directions by the environment such as wind, rain, rivers, and roads. This implies that "Tao" originally meant to surrender oneself to nature. However, in the modern character of "Tao", the bending human form has evolved into the character "首" for "head", and the surroundings have morphed into a character meaning "move", reflecting that the "Tao" of modern generations no longer demands we obey nature but rather that we follow the mind.

Let's look at the evolution of another key word: "听", which means "listen". The traditional character (to the left) contains three elements: ears, eyes, and heart, demonstrating that in the original

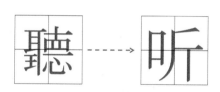

meaning, "listening" was done not only with the ears, but also required visual focus and to be fully attentive with one's heart. The simplified character for listening (to the right) lost the former three listening organs and replaced them with a mouth. Perhaps it is little coincidence that these days you will often hear people complain that people only know how to talk without listening.

Countless examples of word structures conceal philosophical truths. This applies not only to Chinese characters but also to English words, which are rich with meaning. By comparing similar terms, we can highlight the differences between Eastern and Western perspectives. Let's examine the word for "home" in both the East and the West:

The Chinese character for home (家) is composed of a pig under a roof, signifying the importance of livestock, which provides both food and fertilizer for farming. This was the base and the first stage of home. Two other characters, "安" (peace) and "富" (wealth), are intimately related to the concept of home. "安 (peace)" depicts a woman under a roof, symbolizing peace, while "富 (wealth)" shows a jar of wine under a roof, symbolizing wealth. Together, these characters emphasize that the traditional trifecta of Chinese familial bliss—home, peace, and wealth—occurs under the eaves. The common radical of roof serves as the key symbol connecting all aspects of a Chinese home. Traditionally, the most admirable home is one where "four generations live under one roof," known as "四世同堂" in Chinese. Even today, owning a house that accommodates all grown-up children living together remains the dream home for most families. Nowadays, the goal of the Chinese government is to achieve a "小康社会", a moderately prosperous society where homes embody wealth, representing the target of the third stage homes (富) in societal development. The history of Chinese society is vividly displayed by these three characters (家, 安, 富) in sequence.

Now, let's look at the English word "home." The suffix is "me", implying that the base of western home is not a roof covering the whole family but "me". The capital letter "H" is composed of two "I"s connected hand-in-hand. The middle letter "o" stands for "open" or "ocean". Taken together, the Western word "home" is rooted in self and constructed by two equal partners working hand in hand. Western homes are not confined under the roof.

Rather, Westerners often move and change houses following their interest and work, as their home is where their heartbeats reside.

The contrast between the Chinese and Western concepts of "home" reveals a fundamental cultural difference: Chinese culture emphasizes family orientation, while Western culture values individual freedom. Without understanding the archetypes and instincts of the collective unconscious, it is hard to imagine how words created by our ancestors could connect so many life philosophies across different eras and cultures. As embodiments of the soul of life, words instinctively adhere to the collective unconscious and the unified laws of life. Independent of individuals, they objectively record human history and the true essence of life.

2.2 The Roots of Rules

It's interesting to note the similarity in sound between the words "root" and "rules." Both begin with the letter "r," which, in its original Egyptian hieroglyph form, represented a human head. This coincidence suggests that many rules of humanity are defined at the roots of words by the collective human unconscious, as shown by the examples below.

As mentioned in the introduction, the letters in the English words "DOG" and "GOD" are reversed by 180 degrees. DOG and GOD represent two poles of human essence: Dog symbolizes the primitive animal nature from which humanity emerged, while God represents the spiritual

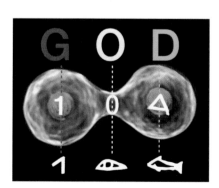

essence to which we aspire. Let's take a closer look at the three letters of GOD:

The tail-letter of GOD, "D," originally derives from the Egyptian hieroglyph for fish and evolved into "delta (Δ)" in the Greek alphabet. The central letter, "O," comes from the hieroglyphic sign for eye and is the initial for "ocean" and "origin." The shape of the letter "O" is also similar to the number "zero." The head-letter of GOD, "G," evolved from the letter "C," which originated from hieroglyph for sling, a primitive stone tool. Its Phoenician letter resembles the number "1," which, according to Yi Jing, The Book of Changes, represents change, while "0" represents origin. "C" and "G" are the starting letters for dynamic words such as create, change, chance, civilization, grow, and go. This composition of the word "GOD," in its Phoenician letter forms, reveals a worldview akin to that espoused in Taoism: "One generates two, two generates three, and three generates infinity." Thus, the universal rules and footprints of life's evolution, or the creation of GOD, are engraved in the roots of the word "GOD."

Much like the Taiji symbol, the structure of each word is formed from life's perfect logic, evident not only in the meaning of each letter but also in their sequence. For example, the initial letter "D" in "DOG" precedes the initial letter "G" in "GOD," suggesting an earlier and later, or lower and higher,

position of DOG and GOD. This pattern is also evident in the sequences of "EVIL" and "LIVE." This cyclical growth pattern, moving from lower to higher, is well illustrated in the "root" of the letter "e"—the human figure in its Egyptian hieroglyph ( ), where the raised arms and the body's two lines depict an upward helical pattern from left to right.

The same helical and reversal pattern seen in DOG and GOD appears in Chinese as well. The conjunction "且", one of the most frequently used characters, means "and." It originates from oracle bone script depicting a penis and was later adapted to mean "ancestor (祖)" when a radical "礻" was added to it. Interestingly, when flipped 180 degrees, "且" becomes the evolved word for "self (自)" and is a key upper component of the word for "nose (鼻)."

The nose is often associated with one's ego, especially in men. This is why a man will point to his nose and say "it's me" when he is happy and proud, but will hit another man's nose when he is angry.

Combining the characters "鼻" (nose) and "祖" (ancestor) forms "鼻祖," meaning the highest authority or the "god" of a school of thought. The evolution from the lower body origin "penis - 且" to the upper body organ "nose - 鼻" representing "self - 自" and then to "鼻祖" like god of authority, exhibits the same reversal and upgrade pattern from DOG to GOD. Moreover, the two lines in both 且 and 自 are similar to those in the human figure ⚇, the archetype of the letter "e." The similarity and common rules among the roots of eastern and western words are simply amazing.

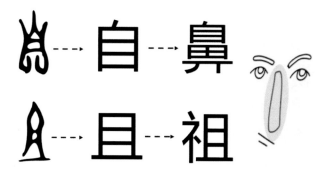

In science, the capital "E" is the symbol for Energy, while the small "e" represents electrons. An atom's structure, which consists of a various number of electrons in orbits revolving around a central nucleus with different energy levels, illustrates a universal life pattern, similar to that of a person orbiting the earth or the earth orbiting the sun.

E, as you may recall, is the archetype of humans. To that we now add its connection to energy, electrons, eggs, Eve, eyes, Earth, ego and everything. Although the primitive form and original meaning of E and e may be forgotten, its archetype has never died, and it has become the most frequently used letter.

The word "Seed" provides another example. The initial letter "S" is the same as in "start," while the last letter "d" is also the last letter in "end." Between "S" and "d" lies a pair of "e" letters, representing the archetype of the male and female couple. This perhaps implies that, in human perception, human is central to all the seeds of life cycles.

Finally, consider a word group that reveals the unified logic of life: she, female, and woman. Within each of these female-related words lies the word of male:

This indicates that every man comes from a mother's body, reflecting the truth in the Taiji symbol: inside every yin (female) lies a yang (male), and vice versa. Likewise, today's avant-garde men often display female qualities, which is not wired situation, but a natural phenomena of life evolution following the universal reversal pattern.

2.3 The Roots of Homophonic Words

The meanings of words are intertwined like strands of pine trees sharing a common root system deep beneath the forest floor. The deeper the roots, the more common patterns are discovered. This nature is rooted in the collective unconscious and archetypes.

Since spoken language precedes written language like deeper roots, even more coincidences can be found among word pronunciations, known as homophony. When I use pinyin input to type Chinese, I often encounter typos due to words that share the same pronunciation. An example of this is the distinct Chinese words "同" meaning "same" and "通" meaning "connected", both pronounced as "tong". Through this, I've observed that many words with identical pronunciations often have similar or related meanings.

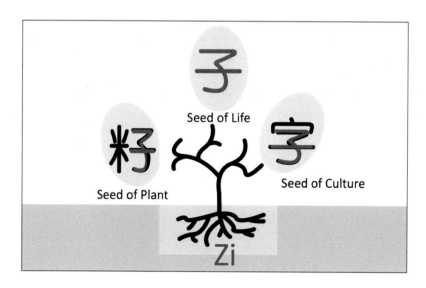

In Chinese, there are three words pronounced as "zi": "籽" means the seed of plant; "子" means "son" or the seed of human; and "字" means "word"—the seed of language and culture. Despite visually distinct characters and separate origins, these words converge in their deeper meanings as "seeds" with the same sound.

Moreover, the common root component among these seeds is once again "子"—the son, the seed of humans. This mirrors the meaning found in the English word "seed," which at its core contains a pair of human figures.

These coincidences sparked my curiosity about the origins of word pronunciations. Across languages, the first vowels often resemble "a" and share the same pronunciation, [a:]. This sound mirrors the cries of many animals and is among the first utterances made by human babies at birth, inherited from our animal ancestors.

Speech predates written language. If we liken the ever-changing history of writing to a branching tree, then pronunciation forms the foundational roots of language, deeper even than the structure of writing. Like a network of seemingly independent trees that are interconnected underground, languages are linked at their roots in the human unconscious. The deeper these collective unconscious prototypes take root, the more evident their shared homology becomes.

In the dense and complex jungle of today's languages and writing systems, the most primitive root is the vowel "a". It not only connects human languages but also extends to the languages of animals.

Following the innate cries at birth, the first word spoken by most human babies is typically to call their mother. This sound is nearly universal across languages: "Ma-Ma." Similarly, the second word often learned is to call their father, which varies slightly between languages. For instance, in English it's typically "papa," in Chinese "baba," and in many African regions, it's pronounced "dada". Despite the consonant variations (B,D,P), the vowel remains [a:].

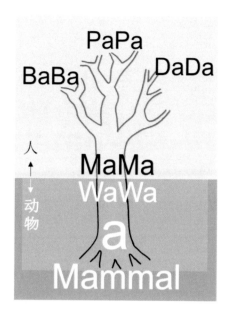

This pattern arises because babies are born from their mothers, so they initially relate more closely to them than to their fathers. The diagram here illustrates how words' sounds branch out from the same linguistic trunk.

Delving into the roots of the English alphabet, I found that five consonants f, u, v, w, and y all originate from a common Egyptian hieroglyph ⌐, which means a "hook" or a hairpin on a woman's head, or a was-scepter as another interpretation. This hieroglyph evolved into the Semitic letter "waw," whose Phoenician form resembles the modern English letter "Y." This shape, resembling a sprouting plant, has become the scientific symbol for the male gene.

Although the original meaning of "waw" is generally forgotten, the consonants f, u, v, w, and y still retain their association with their deep maternal origins and appear in many keywords related to women and birth: female, woman, umbilical cord, vagina, yield, etc. Similar to how the form of the English letter "e" carries the archetypal shapes of a fetus, egg, and universe, the letter "waw" resembles a small animal ("a") in waves of water ("w...w"). Another coincidence in these deeper root connections is that "wa" is the Chinese pronunciation for cry ("哇") and baby ("娃"). It is also the same last syllable in the Chinese name for Eve, "夏娃 (Xia-wa)," and the Chinese equivalent of the goddess "女娲 (Nü-wa)."

This evokes another homophonic coincidence between the Chinese word "我们" for "we" and the English word "women." They sound exactly the same: [women].

These coincidences are no accident but stem from common roots in the deeper layers of sound that connect Eastern and Western cultures. This is the inherited, profound archetype of humanity with common feminine origin—⸙, which evolved into the symbol of divine authority, the scepter in the hands of gods in ancient mythologies.

The story of human evolution engraved in words reaches even further, touching the deep roots shared with animals. The long vowel (oː/uː) of the original Semitic sound of "waw" is the same as the "o" in "vowel" and "wolf." The "O" in its Egyptian origin represents the original "eye," a common form among all animals, mirroring the shapes of cells and eggs.

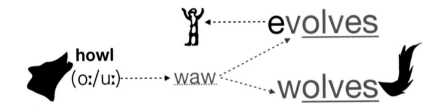

Coincidentally, the plural "wolves" shares its ending with the word "evolves." Furthermore, the howl of a wolf sounds exactly like the original "waw" - [oː/uː]. Interestingly, the tail of "howl" is "owl," one of the most evolved birds, standing in contrast to the primitive wolf.

Carl Jung's insights resonate with these examples of linguistic coincidences, providing evidence for his profound predictions over a century ago:

"In this collective unconscious, we are all linked together, like islands in the sea. We may appear to be separate on the surface, but deep down, at the roots of our being, we are united."

– CARL JUNG

CHAPTER 3

THE ROOTS OF ALPHABETS

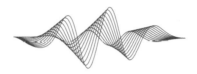

My experience with words has revealed that not all words have an equal chance of exhibiting coincidences. Simpler and more primitive key words, which are used more frequently, are more likely to reveal the common underlying patterns of the collective unconscious. This observation aligns with the fundamental nature of the archetype concept.

With this in mind, I dug into the roots of alphabets at their origins and discovered many a secret embedded within the jungle of words. The following figure shows the twenty-six English letters from higher to lower frequency of use based on information from Wikipedia. To avoid the length of analyzing all the letters in natural alphabet sequence, I will focus on the top three most frequently used key letters as they will bring the most coincidences with significant meanings as typical examples.

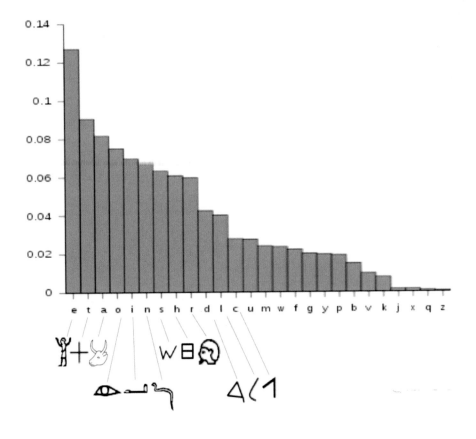

The first three most frequently used letters "e", "t", and "a", in the original Egyptian hieroglyph, are symbols of human, cross, and cow, respectively. They represent the three crucial elements of human origin and evolution: human, god, and animal. Coincidently, these three letters reveal the same nature of three roots of the modern key words DOG and GOD: a fish, the human eye and the God. Now, let's have a closer look at each of these three roots of e, t, and a:

3.1 Letter E, e, The Archetype of Human

Egyptian	Phoenician | Name	Greek	English	Meaning	Modern Words
𓀠	⋀ | He	Eε	E, e	Human	egg, eve, eye, earth, evolve, eternal

1. E is the Eternal Human

Letter "E" is the fifth letter of Latin alphabet, and the most frequently used key letter. It holds significant importance in the writing system. In terms of its original hieroglyphs. "E,e" stands as the sole archetype of a complete human figure 𓀠 with arms open upwards and feet pointing back to the left. The word coincidences around letter "E, e" is the easiest to find and with most significant meanings. While the original meaning of "E,e" as a representation of humans is lost in common sense, its essence, the archetype, persists in the collective unconscious. This archetype is reflected in everything pertaining to human origin, from egg, eye, eve, ego, earth, evolve till eternal.

As shown earlier, the lowercase letter "e" retains a resemblance to a curled fetus and a spiral galaxy, symbolizing the connection between humanity and the universe. Nowadays, the e-world evolves at such a rapid pace that it's difficult to imagine how we ever lived without electricity and electronics. However, very few people pay attention to what this small symbol "e" truly signifies and its crucial role in the process of life's evolution. As evident in the word "evolve," the letter "e" connects the beginning and end of evolution, serving as the ultimate eternal element of life.

2. "e" is electron

In science, "e" is the important symbol for electron. As a natural believer in this philosophy, I find abundant evidence in nature that supports the idea of consistent patterns across the micro- and macro-worlds. With this perspective, I not only perceive humans as small universes but also see electrons within the microcosm as akin to small humans, reflecting the interconnectedness and parallel structures found throughout existence.

The study of word archetypes has provided me with a useful tool for delving into the depths of the collective unconscious, revealing hidden truths through the examination of each letter's original hieroglyph. Same as focusing on key letters, when dealing with complex words, it becomes simple to initiate the analysis by focusing on the first and last letters and the core center which has more weighting factors of significance.

When examining the word "electron," we can see the first three letters, "ele," resembling the defining features of a human face - two eyes flanking a nose. Furthermore, the final letter "n" derived from an Egyptian symbol depicting a snake. As a result, the entire word conjures an image of a human head with a snake's tail.

This is truly fascinating, as it aligns with a recurring divine motif found in ancient mythologies. For instance, in the most renowned Chinese myths, our original ancestors Nv Wa (女娲) and Fu Xi (伏羲) were depicted with human heads and snake tails. In Greek mythology, Medusa, who suffered the unfortunate fate of being raped by the ocean god Poseidon, was transformed into a monstrous creature with a woman's head adorned with snake tails, symbolizing an image of evil to repel evil. In the same way, we can find in the name of western goddess Eve bearing resemblance to "ele" and "eye." Moreover, she was tempted by a snake, hinting at the notion that the snake was the source of humanity's original sin.

In fact, electrons orbiting the nuclei within an atom serve as the micro-archetype of humans on Earth, while the Earth itself, orbiting the sun within the universe, embodies the same macro-archetype of the whole universe.

3. "E" is Energy

Now, let us explore the word "energy" which was represented by capital letter "E" in science.

By examining the roots of its constituent letters in their original hieroglyphs: Energy is formed by six letters, with the first three letters "ene" resembling the same pattern of "ele" in "electron," hinting at a shared motif of a human face. On the other hand, the final letter "Y" as the symbol of male gene, derives from the Egyptian hieroglyph of a hook, representing the "Was Scepter" in ancient Egyptian religion, symbolizing power and dominion. This symbol was associated with Egyptian deities like Khnum and Set, as well as the pharaoh.

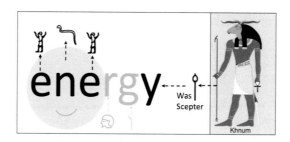

Despite the fact that the original significance of E, e as representing the primitive human has faded from the consciousness of most people, this pair of original human archetypes not only persists but also remains the most commonly used letter in the modern world. It serves as the foundation for numerous crucial words, as exemplified below:

Earth, Eve, Eye, Ear, Egg, Ego, Eat, Evolution, Equation, Eternal, Ether, Easter, Ever, Electric, Electronics, Energy, Empower, Emperor, Expert, Element, Elephant, Elk, Election,

Elevate, Elevator, Expand, Erase, Escape, Error, Enough, The, Be, Me, He, She, Ape, Age, Here, There, Live, Life, Love, See, Observe, Sense, Science, Universe, Space, Time, Evolve...

The word E, e holds a wide and profound influence within the depths of our unconscious, dominates the world, much like the way humanity exerts dominance over the Earth and, perhaps in the future, the entire universe.

Hope this demonstration, featuring the No.1 key letter in its archetypal form as a human, gives you an idea of how easily we can gain a true sense of the collective unconscious pattern in the creation of words in general. Now, let us move to the 2nd most frequently used letter "T, t", a sacred "cross" in its archetypal hieroglyph. You can tell already how important this letter related to humanity.

3.2 Letter T, t, The Archetype of Sacred Cross

Proto-Canaanite	Phoenician | Name	English	Meaning	Modern Words
†	+ |Taw	T, t	Cross, Ten	The, This, That, There, Time, Thought, Tooth, Ten

The letter "T" is the twentieth letter in Latin alphabet and the final letter in the Semitic abjads, including Phoenician. It ranks as the second most frequently used letter after "e." The origin of Proto-Canaanite symbol for "T" depicted a cross, which later evolved into the Phoenician letter "Taw" signifying a tally mark and unity. This sacred symbol is integral to numerous key words, such as "the," which happens to be the most commonly used word in the English language. Additionally, words like "time," "ten," "this," "that," "there," "thought," "teach," "target," "task," and many more derive their profound meaning from the original archetype of the sacred cross, still resonating within them.

1. T is Time:

In the realm of science, "T" and "t" serve as the prevailing symbols denoting time, effectively expanding our perception from the visible three-dimensional space into the concealed fourth dimension. Time, as a concept of immense significance, holds sway over our daily lives, molds our experiences, and carries profound implications across numerous domains of human existence. For examples, time provides a way to measure and organize events, durations, and sequences. It is through the progression of time that transformations occur, whether in nature, society, or personal experiences. Time plays a fundamental role in various scientific disciplines. The concept of time has led to breakthroughs in our understanding of the universe, the nature of reality, and the laws that govern it.

When exploring the essence of the word "time" and delving into its archetypal letters, we uncover a wealth of intricate concepts intertwined within it. For example, the tail, or the genesis, of "time" is the

letter "e," which symbolizes the eternal human. This evolves through "m," representing water, grows into the extended "i," symbolizing an arm as key initial of intelligence, and culminates in the head-letter "t," the sacred cross representing the spirit of the soul. Each letter records a key milestone of human evolution history, giving existence and meaning to the concept of time.

2. T is Ten

The Phoenician letter "T," also known as Taw "+," symbolizes a tally mark system for counting. This counting system is believed to have originated from the primitive practice of using our ten fingers, with five on each hand.

As a result, a tally mark was created using four vertical lines accompanied by a diagonal line intersecting it, effectively representing the number five. By combining two sets of fives, a ten was formed.

It is intriguing to note that, in Chinese, the symbol "+" not only represents "addition" but also a character for number ten. Similarly, the cross symbol and the number ten hold sacred significance in various aspects. They are associated with perfection and hold symbolic value in many cultural and religious contexts. The phrase "十全十美 (perfect 10)" is often used colloquially to refer to something or someone that is considered flawless, outstanding, or of the highest quality. It can be applied to various aspects, such as beauty, performance, or achievement.

Delving into the origin of the word "ten" in its underlying archetypal letters, we encounter once again the repeated motif of the divine human with the tail of a snake, same as the Nv Wa and Fu Xi in Chinese folk tales and Medusa in Greek Mythology.

3. T is Thought

T is the first and last letter of word "thought", which is the most special thing of human that empowered him with unstoppable creation on Earth. Thought is as complex and as sacred as human himself as well as the representation of letter T.

Let's explore the formation of the word "thought" with its original archetypal elements. Given its length of seven letters, let's focus on the first and last letter for a quick glimpse of an intriguing coincidence in contrast to the Chinese word "思想" for thought, which reveals an interesting cultural difference between Western and Eastern perspectives.

† ⋯ Thought ⋯ † 思想

The Western concept of thought begins and ends with the letter "T," symbolizing the sacred cross, while the two Chinese characters share a common base, "心," meaning the heart. This highlights a major cultural difference: Western thought tends to be more rational and systematic, while Eastern thought is more intuitive and spontaneous. However, at the depths of thought, the sacred cross and the heart are interconnected rather than separate.

Another fascinating coincidence lies in the resemblance between T's Phoenician letter "Taw" and the Chinese character "Tao" (道). Variations of "Taw" exist across different languages, such as Tau or Tav, but the core element "Ta" remains unchanged. Examining the hieroglyphic representation of "Ta," we find a motif depicting a sacred cow. Additionally, "Ta" is the pronunciation of "他," equivalent to the English "He," which ends with the

letter "e," symbolizing humanity. While "He" is a pronoun for human, it often used in the Bible to represent God.

This coincidence implies a profound philosophy: the ultimate roots of the rules in nature and life, embodied in "Taw" and "Tao," are defined by two ends of human "Ta "—the animal roots from the earth and the sacred cross from heaven. These connections transcend mere coincidence and reflect the deep interplay within our collective unconscious across diverse cultures. It's the same pattern we see in the beginning and ending letters of words "dog" and "god".

4. T is an Altar

It is truly captivating to observe another intriguing coincidence between a Chinese character "示" and the Western letter "T." The Chinese character "示," pronounced as "shi," holds the same pronunciation as the word for number ten, "十." Interestingly, The character "示" traces its origin back to the earliest oracle hieroglyph, sharing exactly the same form as the letter "T" and representing an Altar.

Proto-Canaanite   English | Oracle   Modern

The intricate relationship between the letter "T" and the Chinese character "示" is just another example of how the tree of life intertwines deeply at its roots. Just as the letter "T" evolves into numerous words carrying sacred meanings, the Chinese character "示" became a radical that leads to a multitude of words, each preserving the original meaning of an Altar. These include words like "神祇" (god), "福" (happiness), "禄" (wellness), "祥" (good luck), and many others.

As we observed previously, the key letter "e" reigns supreme in the world. Similarly, we witness the illuminating and unifying power of the letter "T," which inspires and delights the essence of life. Below, you'll find a concise list of words beginning with "T" and ending with "t," reaffirming the notion that the roots of our collective unconscious not only reside within our conscious minds but continue to expand across time and space, towards a harmonious and interconnected universe.

> To, Two, Three, Twelve, The, This, That, There, Time, Ten, Thought, Teach, Talk, Tell, Term, Terminate, Tech, Tele, Template, Temperature, Tooth, Together, Toward, Top, Tower, etc…About, Light, Delight, Spirit, Great, Let, Get, Eat, Net, Bet, Neat, Quiet, Ant, Cat, Bat, etc.

Before moving to the third key letter, I would like to highlight an intriguing coincidence involving the first two most frequently used letters, E and T, which symbolize "human" and "divine" respectively. Together, they create a unified depiction of humanity with its inherent divine nature. This connection reminds me of the renowned American film, E.T., a groundbreaking science fiction movie that shattered box office records. The storyline revolves around the authentic and profound friendship between a young boy and an extraterrestrial being who lands on Earth, reflecting the cosmic connection embodied by the letters E and T, representing the human and divine. Beyond the remarkable technical aspects and performances, I believe that a deeper, hidden reason for the historical success of this film lies in its powerful name, E.T. —the resonance of its archetypal significance with the hearts of modern humans.

3.3 Letter A, a, The Archetype of Holy Cow

Egyptian	Phoenician | Name	English	Meaning	Modern Words
🐄	✗ | Aleph	**A, a**	OX, Cow	Animal, Ant, Ape, Ancient, Africa, Asia, America, Australia

"A,a" is the first letter of Latin alphabet and the third most frequently used key letter. It holds a significant position as the first letter in nearly all languages and serves as the initial vowel. The origin of the letter "A" can be traced back to the Egyptian Hieroglyph depicting the head of a cow or an ox, which later evolved into the first Phoenician letter known as Aleph. Subsequently, it transformed into the Greek letter Alpha.

The letter "A" has always intrigued me, especially in the context of naming individuals, places, nations, and continents. It seems to unconsciously convey a sense of being first, original, and ancient. Consider the names of the four original races—Africa, Asia, America, and Australia—all of which begin and end, with the letter "A,a." These words embody the profound significance of the archetypal letter "a" for animal, much like life carries ancestral genes within its cells.

Let's delve deeper into more fascinating facts about the letter "a," derived from collective unconscious perceptions.

1. A is the First Vowel

"A" holds significance as it is not only the initial letter in all human languages but also the first vowel. This importance arises from the fact that sound produces written language, and thus has deeper roots in words. While humans primarily communicate through written words, most animals communicate through sounds. It is intriguing to observe that the first vowel, "a," commonly pronounced as /ɑː/ such as in Chinese Pinyin, represents the most prevalent sound among mammals. Interestingly, at times when I hear the calls of frogs, ducks, and birds, their sounds bear a striking resemblance to the cries of human babies.

In the Chinese language, vowels are referred to as "元音" (yuányīn), meaning "the original sound," or "母音" (mǔyīn), meaning "the mother's sound." In contrast, consonants are called "辅音" (fǔyīn), meaning "facilitating sound," or "父音" (fùyīn), meaning "the father's sound," as they follow the vowel. Interestingly, the names of Chinese ancestors reflect this dichotomy. The goddess "女娲" (Nüwa) ends with the vowel "a," while the god "伏羲" (Fuxi) sounds similar to "父系" (fùxì), meaning patriarchy or paternal line.

In comparison to the archetypal letter "e" representing humans, the letter "a" has a deeper connection to animals, symbolized by the head of a holy cow. This connection is further illustrated by the universal sound /a:/ made by humans, which is common among all mammals. Additionally, the first universal language of humans, such as the calling of "ma-ma," shares the same initial as the word "mammal."

The cow's female nature represents humanity's common female ancestors, which explains why the names of the first four generations of Greek goddesses, Gaia, Rhea, Hera, and Athena, all carry the common tail-letter of "a" representing the same maternal root of the holy cow.

Athena Ma
Hera Mather
Rhea Mama
Gaia Mammal Cow

2. A is the Blood Type of OX

I used to wonder why the four blood types are symbolized by ABO instead of ABCD. However, upon reflecting on the original meanings of the letters, I discovered that the choice of ABO embodies a collective unconscious instinctively adhering to unified archetypal logic. Different personalities associated with various blood types have evolved along with the characteristics embedded in the original meanings of the letters A, B, and O.

The universal blood type O likely originates from the primordial ocean water, where all life evolved. Thus, individuals with blood type O tend to have balanced, inclusive, and open-minded personalities. Blood type B individuals share characteristics with birds and bees: they are social, harmonious, and family-oriented. In contrast, those with blood type A are often known for being persistent, stubborn, practical, and down-to-earth. My entire family, except for myself, has blood type A. I remember during arguments, no one would back down, prompting my mom to say, "Where did these tempers of an ox in our family come from?!"

After learning that the archetype of the letter A is a cow or ox's head, I realized this explains my mom's question. The stubborn personality and strong temper come from the blood type A, the far origin of the ox. While goddesses inherit common female genes from the cow, the later fathers and sons of their descendants also carry the letter A in their names and exhibit the temperaments of blood type A of the ox. This explains also the coincidence of the four continents of human origin—Africa, Australia, Asia, and America—all start and end with the letter A. Similarly, major paternal ancestors such as Adam, Apollo, Abraham, and Alexander all have the initial letter A in their names.

America
Asia
Australia
Africa

Alexandra
Abraham
Apollo
Adam

OX

If you pay attention, you will be fascinated to discover how many names of continents, nations, and species carry the head and tail of the letter "A," connecting to its ancient nature. Here again is a short list from which you can feel the connection to these holy roots:

Alpha, Africa, Aisa, America, Arizona, Australia, Madagascar, India, China, Arabia, Albania, Argentina, Armenia, Angela, Artemisia, Alexsandra, Adam, Apollo, Area, Arena, Arctic, Antarctic, Ancient, Animal, Ant, Antelope, Ape, Apple, Archaea, Agave, Acers, Acacia,...

3. Continued Worship of The Holy Cow

In addition to the names that carry the roots of the letter "A," cows have been worshipped and are still considered sacred in many cultures.

The emblem of Madagascar has the head of a cow as the base from which the sun rises, with the body of their land at the center. This intriguing connection echoes the history conveyed by the letter "A." Similarly, India, with the letter "a" being the tail of its name, reveals a parallel significance. In Hinduism, cows are held in high regard and revered as symbols of life and fertility.

In ancient Egypt, cows were linked to the goddess Hathor, representing love, motherhood, and joy. Hathor was often depicted with cow horns or as a cow herself. In ancient Greece and Rome, cows were associated with fertility and agricultural deities like Demeter and Ceres.

According to Chinese tradition, it is believed that all Chinese people descended from two direct ancestors: Yan (炎) and Huang (黄), who are two grandsons of Nv Wa (女娲) and Fu Xi (伏羲). As introduced earlier, Nv Wa and Fu Xi are depicted with human heads and snake tails. The elder brother Yan, being the ancestor of agriculture, is represented with the image of a cow's head and a human body.

Yan (炎帝)　　Hathor

To conclude this chapter, let's look back at the first three most frequently used letters together, E, T, and A. These three letters are indeed the key archetypal elements that define the meaning of life in connection with the universe. E, T, and A constitute the three components of the word "EAT," the base of existence and survival for all animals. While "E" dominates the world as human, "T" enlightens the divine spirits, letter "A" connects the roots of beginning and the end of life.

In the table below, I have summarized the original archetypes of the 26 English letters. Throughout my book, I often spontaneously refer to a key word in terms of its archetypes to gain new insights into its deeper meanings. If you are interested in exploring the collective unconscious world of alphabets further, please check out my ebook on Amazon, "The Archetypal Letters."

Letter	Hieroglyph	meaning	Letter	Hieroglyph	Meaning	English	Hieroglyph	Meaning
A		OX Head	H		Fence Hedjet	P		Mouth
B		House	I/J		Arm	Q		nod
C/G		Sling	K		Hand	R		Head
D		Fish	L		OX Goad Cattle Prod	S		tooth
E		Human	M		Water	T		Cross
F, U, V W, Y		Hook Scepter	N		Sanke	X		Cross
			O		Eye	Z		Manacle Weapon

CHAPTER 4

SCIENTIFIC SYMBOLS

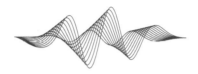

Drawing from experiences where coincidences among keywords and alphabets often emerge, I began to explore key scientific symbols, initially believed to be chosen by individual scientists. As expected, I found that many symbols are not solely the creation of an individual's conscious mind but also manifestations of the collective unconscious. Here, I will outline some instinctive connections between scientific symbols and the original meanings of archetypal letters—connections that remain significant even though the archetypes of these letters have long been forgotten.

4.1 Chemical Elements

To date, there are 118 confirmed chemical elements. These elements are organized in the periodic table, ranging from hydrogen (H, atomic number 1) to oganesson (Og, atomic number 118). I believe that, much like the letters of the alphabet, we can uncover endless coincidences among chemical symbols that reveal how the collective unconscious guides the choice of each name and symbol. To narrow our focus while maintaining the significance of our examples, we will examine the three most abundant elements in the universe and the three key elements in the human body, paralleling our analysis of the most frequently used letters.

The three most abundant elements in the universe are hydrogen (H), helium (He), and oxygen (O), comprising approximately 74%, 24%, and 1% of the total elements, respectively. Together, these three elements make up 99% of the universe. Similarly, in the human body, the three most abundant elements are oxygen (O), carbon (C), and hydrogen (H), making up about 65%, 18%, and 10% of the total elements, respectively, summing to roughly 93%.

In this chapter, we will delve into these four key chemical symbols: H, He, O, and C, to uncover the secrets that lie deep within the archetypes of the collective unconscious.

1. H is Hydrogen

H is the symbol for Hydrogen, the first element in the periodic table, and the most abundant element in the universe. As the primary constituent of stars, including our Sun, hydrogen has played a central role in the universe's formation and evolution. Shortly after the Big Bang, the universe was predominantly composed of hot, dense hydrogen gas. As it expanded and cooled, hydrogen atoms coalesced into clouds, eventually giving rise to galaxies, stars, and other celestial structures—marking the beginning of cosmic evolution.

An intriguing observation is the three-line structure of the letter "H," which is similar to the Chinese character "天" (sky). This resemblance is notable considering that English is written horizontally while traditional Chinese is written vertically. The three lines of "H" mirror the connection of sky and earth with humanity in between. This concept echoes the universal three stages of development described in the "Yi Jing" (Book of Changes).

^1H气 ^2H氘 ^3H氚

Hydrogen has three isotopes: 1H, 2H, and 3H. Coincidentally, the Chinese characters for hydrogen's three isotopes—气, 氘, and 氚—share a similar structural pattern. The common top radical "气" signifies "air," while the bottom radicals feature 1, 2, and 3 lines, symbolizing three vital elements: air (丿), humanity (人), and water (川, river). Moreover, the Chinese character for Hydrogen, "氢," contains the bottom root "工." When rotated 90 degrees, it resembles the letter "H," considering the different tradition of vertical and horizontal writing.

Egyptian	Phoenician | Name*	Greek	English	Meaning	Modern Words
⧠ 𓀋	日 |Het |Heth	日	H, h	Light, Sun, Universe	He, His, Home, Heaven, Heart, Head, Hand, Have

Let's explore the archetype of the letter "H" in its Egyptian origin. H is the 8th letter in the Latin alphabet and the 9th most frequently used letter. The Egyptian hieroglyph for "H" has taken on various interpretations over time, such as a fence, courtyard, and a twisted wick. Initially, these divergent meanings seemed puzzling, but after years of study, a coherent understanding has emerged. The most fitting interpretation of "H" in its original form appears to be "light," the fundamental source of life. This interpretation connects the meanings of fence and courtyard (sunlight outside the house) and the twisted wick (candlelight inside the house).

An intriguing coincidence lies in the Phoenician letter for H, which closely resembles the Chinese character "日" (sun). Additionally, the Phoenician names for H, such as "Het" or "Heth," share the common initial "He," coincidentally the symbol for Helium, the second element, whose Greek name also means "sun."

For simplicity and consistency, I will use the twisted wick "ᛦ" as the original hieroglyph and archetype for "H." It represents light, enlightenment, the helix foundation of DNA, and, in the grandest sense, the ultimate home of life—the solar system and the universe.

Thus, it becomes evident that the choice of "H" as the symbol for hydrogen was not random but rather guided by the collective unconscious to convey its significance as the fundamental element of life, the light from the universe. This profound connection is reflected in many related keywords such as Heaven, Hell, Home, Heart, Head, Hand, Have, Has, Hi, and High.

2. He is Helium

Helium, the second lightest and second most abundant element in the universe after Hydrogen, derives its name from Greek origins, signifying the "sun," because it was first detected as a yellow spectral line from sunlight. So "He" was chosen as the symbol of Helium.

In cosmology, helium is closely related to the Sun and other stars and plays a crucial role in stellar processes. It is produced in stars through the process of nuclear fusion, where hydrogen atoms fuse to form helium, releasing enormous amounts of energy. This process not only fuels the Sun and allows it to shine but also contributes to the creation of heavier elements in stars. Helium's presence and production in the Sun and other stars are fundamental to stellar evolution and the overall dynamics of the cosmos.

Coincidentally, "He" is the third-person pronoun for humans and is also used to represent God in the Bible. Furthermore, He = H + e, symbolizing sunlight (H) and human (e), aligning with the concept of the sun god, such as the Egyptian Sun God Ra and the Greek Sun God Apollo.

Amidst the web of coincidences surrounding H, e, and He, I've discovered an intriguing connection between the Chinese word for helium (氦) and He, similar to the word for hydrogen (氢) and H. The top radical of "氦" (He) shares the same "air" radical as "氢" (H). The bottom part of "氦" is the Chinese character "亥," which means pig. In the same way that "工," an upright "H," appears at the bottom of 氢 (H), The body of "亥" has a pattern resembling a helix, the common archetype of the hieroglyphs of H (⚡) and e (⚡).

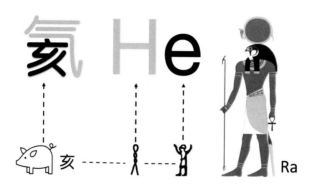

In addition, the name "He" and the character "氦" contain the same archetypal image as Ra, the ancient Egyptian sun god, who is typically depicted with an animal head crowned with a solar disk, emphasizing his association with the sun, light, and creation. This makes "He" a fitting symbol for helium.

3. O is the Eye

Oxygen (O) is the third most abundant element in the universe and the most abundant element in the human body. When we compare the top three abundant elements in the universe (H, He, O) with those in the human body (O, C, H), an interesting universal reversal pattern emerges, reminiscent of the reversal seen in the words DOG and GOD, as well as the word "seed".

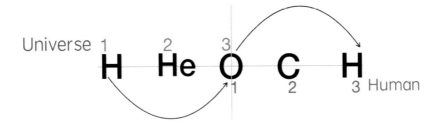

Universe 1   2   3

H   He   O   C   H

                    1   2   3 Human

Notably, in this pattern, the symbol for oxygen (O), the most vital element for life, sits at the center of the key elements in both the universe and the human body. The form of O is a circle or zero, and its archetype, such as in the Egyptian hieroglyph, is an eye.

Egyptian	Phoenician | Name	English	Meaning	Modern Words
⬮	O | eyn	O,o	Eye	Observe, Look, Wow, Oh, Origin, Ocean

Many modern keywords still carry the original meaning of "O," such as ocean, observe, and origin. The eye is an organ with a common shape among all animals. It actually shares the same shape with a cell, an egg, the Earth, and even the universe when viewed with a black hole at the center. The eye is also considered the window to the

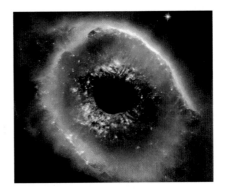

human soul, as depicted by the eye of the Sun God Ra in Egyptian mythology.

Given these broad and profound connections to life, it's hard to imagine a better symbol for oxygen than the letter "O." The choice of this symbol underscores the instinctive wisdom of the collective unconscious.

4. C is the Creator

Carbon (C) is the second most abundant element in the human body and the fourth most abundant element in the universe. It serves as the foundation for all organic compounds, playing a crucial role in sustaining life on Earth. Its scientific symbol, the letter "C," carries symbolic meanings: while "O" represents "Origin," "C" represents "Create and Change."

Egyptian	Phoenician |Name*	Greek	English	Meaning	Modern Words
)	⌐ | Gimel	Γγ	C,G	Staff Sling	Create, Change, Chance, Grow, God

The archetype of the letter C in its Egyptian hieroglyph resembles a primitive stone tool, symbolizing the beginning of human civilization. The Phoenician letter for C resembles the modern number "1," also symbolizing change comparing to number "0". Letter G, the initial letter of words like God, Grow, and Go, evolved from letter C, carrying out its nature of "Create and Change".

Coincidently, one of carbon's unique properties is its ability to change, from the softest graphite to the hardest natural material, diamond. There are as many as 10 million carbon compounds, serving as the material basis for the diverse forms of life on Earth.

In Chinese characters, the original meaning of carbon is reflected in its formation, "碳" for Carbon is composed of rock (石) on the left, mountain (山) on the top right, and ash (灰) at the bottom right. Within the ash "灰" lies the fire "火", and within fire resides the human "人", echoing the archetypal pattern seen in "He," and "氦."

The structure of the word "碳 (C)" evokes imagery of a volcanic eruption with rocks and ashes bursting forth. It supplies fundamental trace elements necessary for human life and supports the ecosystem for life's evolution. This image resonates with creation myths, such as the biblical account of forming man from the dust of the ground. It mirrors the fact that Carbon's capacity to form a wide array of compounds and create polymers at Earth's temperatures is crucial for life's creation.

In the human body, Carbon constitutes approximately 18.5% of our mass and plays vital roles in organic chemistry and biochemistry through functional groups like -CO (carbonyl group) and -OH (hydroxyl group).

Deep within our cell nuclei, carbon compounds like ribose and deoxyribose resemble vivid human figures, connecting scientific structures to human archetypes. Even more fascinating that I found the archetype of the "Lamed" original human from the image of Deoxyribose.

Ribose

Deoxyribose

The word "GOD" contains symbolic connections such as GO=CO, where the tail-letter "D" symbolizes a fish, an archetype representing a common ancestor, revealing the secret of how God created humans.

Ultimately, the common sound of crater and creator connects and encircles scientific discoveries and religious beliefs, revealing the profound interplay of collective unconscious archetypes in human understanding.

4.2 Biology Symbols

1. Blood Type

Previously, I highlighted the interesting choice of using ABO instead of ABCD to represent the four major blood types: A, B, AB, and O. Understanding the archetypal meanings of the letters A, B, and O reveals that they instinctively reflect familiar personalities and temperaments associated with each blood type:

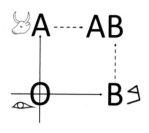

- Letter "A", originating from the head of a cow or ox in its archetype, brings out the bull-like temperament of those with blood type A: persistent, stubborn, practical, and down-to-earth.

- Letter "B", derived from the original hieroglyph meaning "house," represents animals like "Bee" and "Bird" with instinctive talent to build home. People with blood type B often display characteristics common to bees and birds: they are social, harmonious, easygoing, and family-oriented.

- Letter "O", with its archetype as an eye, represents life's common origins, as seen in words like "Ocean" and "Origin." Statistically, blood type O is more common among Africans, Indians, and Australian Indigenous peoples, geographical regions from which human populations originally spread. Blood type O, as the "universal" blood donor type that can be received by any other blood type, signifies inclusive characteristics. It's possible that the ultimate origin of blood type O came from ocean water, as life originates from the sea. Like a cell dividing, blood type O may have split into two opposite types: A and B. Eventually, A and B merged into AB, and finally, when all the types mixed evenly, they were reunified back into Type O.

This perspective not only aligns with the symbolic meanings of the letters but also reflects the interconnected nature of human evolution and the diversity of our genetic heritage.

2. DNA & RNA

DNA (Deoxyribonucleic Acid) and RNA (Ribonucleic Acid) are essential molecules in the biology of all living organisms. Together, DNA and RNA form the fundamental genetic and functional framework of life, with DNA holding the genetic blueprint and RNA facilitating the expression of these genes into proteins.

First, let's examine the structure of letters in the appearance of DNA and RNA: Both DNA and RNA contain the same two tail letters, "NA," which in their original hieroglyphs represented a snake and a cow head, respectively. These symbols frequently appear in key words related to humanity, such as "Man," which also contains the same two tails of sacred animal roots. In Chinese, there is an idiom "牛鬼蛇神," which literally means "the ghost of a cow and the deity of a snake," used as a general representation of evil spirits. Coincidentally, the names of human races—such as Asian, Caucasian, African, American, Mongolian, Malayan, Ethiopian—all end with the letters "an," reminiscent of the two roots of DNA and RNA, but in reversed form.

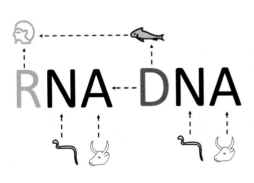

The archetype of the first letter in DNA, "D," was a fish, the known common direct ancestor of humans, as seen in the word pair "DOG" and "GOD," symbolizing the head of the dog and the tail of God. In contrast, the first letter of RNA, "R," has evolved to represent the human head. Thus, the structure of DNA and RNA not only records our deep animal roots but also the transformation process in converting genetic information in the roots of DNA into the protein of RNA.

Secondly, let delving into deeper level of the function and structure of DNA: It is a double-stranded helix composed of nucleotides, each containing a sugar (deoxyribose), a phosphate group, and one of four nitrogenous bases: adenine (A), thymine (T), cytosine (C), or guanine (G). DNA stores genetic information and serves as a blueprint for building and maintaining an organism. It contains instructions for development, functioning, growth, and reproduction. The archetypes of the four letters A, T, C, and G are also fascinating:

- **A** (Cow Head): Represents the earthly animal root.
- **T** (Sacred Cross): Represents the heavenly human spirit.
- **C** (Stone Tool): Symbolizes creation and change.
- **G** (Evolved from C): Indicates growth.

It is fascinating to find how well these archetypes of letters match the functions of symbols assigned to them. Once again, demonstrate that the choice of these symbols is never random but carefully designed and planned by the inherited wisdom of the collective unconscious, reflecting the continuity of our DNA blueprints. It is not difficult to understand if you can imagine the earth, the sun, the stars, and the entire universe as giant beings, evolving from small entities like "e" to "egg," "eye," "eve," "earth," all the way towards the "eternal."

3. Chromosomes

XX and XY represent female and male chromosomes, respectively. These symbols reveal several significant insights into the nature of genetic differences between the sexes.

Firstly, the structure of the letters themselves reflects the differences in genetic makeup: XX is perfectly symmetrical, while XY is not. This mirrors the actual structure of the chromosomes and suggests why female genes often have advantages over male genes in general.

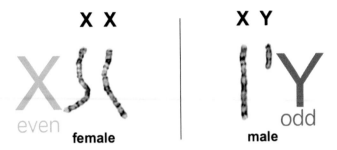

X X

even

female

X Y

odd

male

The structure of the letters X and Y also aligns with the traditional Chinese theory of Yin-Yang for female and male nature: X, composed of two strokes (an even number), represents Yin, or the female nature, while Y, composed of three strokes (an odd number), signifies Yang, or the male nature.

The archetype of the letter X means "ten," a perfect number, symbolizing the original perfection of the female human gene. Meanwhile, the archetype of Y is the was-scepter, signifying authority, derived from the hieroglyph of a woman's hair hook (𐪍), indicating that man originates from woman, as reflected in the female words "wo<u>man</u>, fe<u>male</u>, and s<u>he</u>," inside of each we find "man, male, and he". These all explain consistently why the female gene has an advantage over the male gene, as a whole versus a part.

An additional interesting coincidence is found in the symbols for bird genetics, where WZ represents the female bird and ZZ represents the male bird. In contrast to humans, the symbol for the male bird gene (ZZ) is more symmetrical than WZ, reflecting the fact that male birds often display more vibrant colors and may have advantages over female birds, the reversal pattern of human genetics. Furthermore, the alphabetical sequence of W and Z, with W preceding X and Z following Y, subtly indicates that birds typically have longer lifespans than humans.

WXYZ

阴 阳

雌性特征
(阴)

雄性特征
(阳)

These patterns and coincidences are not random but are guided by the collective unconscious, which follows a perfect logic and rationale beyond individual consciousness.

4.3 Mathematical Symbols

1. "e" is the Irrational and Transcendental Human

Besides being the symbol of electron and energy, The letter "e" is also a significant scientific symbol representing an irrational and transcendental number, approximately equal to 2.71828. It is commonly referred to as a "natural" constant, even though it is not a natural number like 1, 2, or 3. It is defined as the base of the natural logarithm, denoted as ln(x).

Personally, I have always been fascinated by irrational and transcendental numbers such as "pi" and "e," and I am not alone in this fascination. When Google filed for its initial public offering (IPO) in 2004, it announced its intention to raise 2,718,281,828 USD, essentially "e" billion dollars. This connection further reinforces my belief in the "natural growth" of Google. This belief stems from the meaning of the head letters in Google's name, "Go," and its tail letter, "e," symbolizing the unstoppable nature of humanity.

There are intriguing features of the number "e" that are closely tied to life. For instance:

- Exponential function: One fascinating characteristic of "e" is that the exponential function e^x is equal to itself, expressed as d/dx(e^x) = e^x. Personally, I perceive this as akin to the pattern of "dog & god," representing the recurring life cycles embodied by "e." It serves as a symbol of the most primal aspects of humanity, still present and intertwined in every facet of the modern world and life. This quality of "e" is truly irrational and transcendental, surpassing our conscious reasoning and imagination.

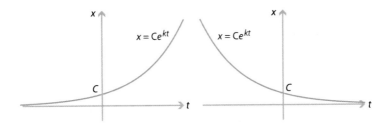

- Exponential growth: The number "e" exhibits a remarkable property in the realm of exponential growth. It serves as the base rate shared by all continuously growing processes, where an initial amount increases at a consistent rate over time. Analysts employ this mathematical concept to make predictions about the future. For instance, under a continuously compounded interest rate, the amount of money in an account will grow by a factor of "e" over a unit of time. Furthermore, this concept finds applications in social and life sciences, such as predicting the expected population of a city, the trajectory of an infectious disease, the amount of a drug remaining in a patient's bloodstream, or the decay of certain radioactive isotopes.

- Golden Rational: The golden spiral is a logarithmic spiral, which has many awe-inspiring names, such as growth spiral, an eternal line, the marvelous spiral, etc., due to its self-similar spiral pattern that often appears in nature. The logarithmic spiral with the polar equation : r = a * e^(kθ), where e is the "e" is the base of the natural logarithm, θ is the angle in radians and r is the distance from the origin. When the constant k is related to the golden ratio (Φ) such that k = ln(Φ) ≈ 0.48121182505960347. it generates the polar equation for a golden spiral: r = a *e^(0.481211825059603470θ). The golden spiral is a unique and visually striking spiral found abundantly in nature, art, and architecture. It grows larger while maintaining its shape through a constant expansion factor, approximately 1.618, the golden ratio. This mesmerizing pattern has fascinated artists, architects, and mathematicians alike for centuries, inspiring the creation of timeless masterpieces that incorporate its elegant proportions. The golden spiral's prevalence in the natural world, from seashells to galaxies, adds to its mystique and reinforces its status as a symbol of harmony and aesthetic perfection. To me, the root of all these wonders of science and nature, lies in the magic archetypal form of human, as revealed in the form of eternal letter "e" itself.

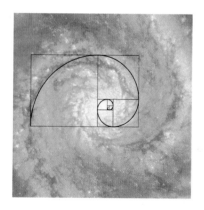

2. I am the Imaginary

"Knowledge is more important than knowledge, knowledge is limited. Imagination encircles the world."

−EINSTEIN.

Egyptian	Phoenician Name	English	Meaning	Modern Words
▱	𐤉 Yod	I,i/J,j	Arm	I, In, If, Is, Intelligence, Imagine, Inspiration

The letter "I" is the 9th letter in the Latin alphabet, and its original archetype in Egyptian hieroglyphs was an arm. In comparison to the earlier letter "e," depicted as a complete human figure " ☥ ," the letter "i" resembles a human figure with the head standing out on top, suggesting an advanced human with an independent mind. This explains why key words such as "intelligence," "imagination," and "inspiration" all begin with the letter "i." The extended arms differentiate humans fundamentally from animals, allowing intelligence to grow from the ability to stand upright and to free the arms for using tools.

As the initial letter of "imagination," "I" is fittingly chosen to represent the imaginary unit in mathematics—a foundational concept that plays a crucial role in various mathematical and scientific contexts. It enables the understanding and analysis of phenomena involving both real and imaginary components.

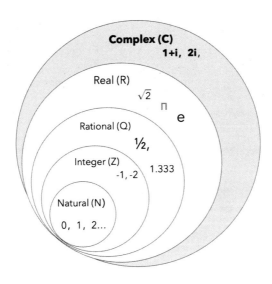

The imaginary unit "i" is defined as the square root of -1, where $i^2 =$ -1. Initially conceived purely from logical reasoning, it had no basis in physical reality but has since led to numerous practical applications. The concept of complex numbers extends the realm of numbers from natural numbers, through rational and real numbers, to complex numbers, thereby expanding our knowledge from natural instincts, through rationality and realism, to a complete understanding of both visible and invisible, conscious and unconscious worlds. This expansion is thanks to the power of the "I" as the symbol of extended arm and imagination.

A complex number (c) is typically denoted as c = a + bi, where "a" represents the real component and "bi" signifies the imaginary component. This notation allows numbers to be visually depicted on the complex plane, with the real part plotted along the x-axis and the imaginary part along the y-axis. The symbols "Re" and "Im" are used to represent the real and imaginary axes, respectively.

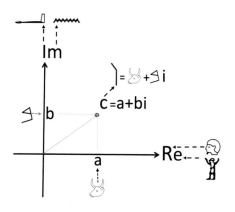

Examining the coordinate labels, the real axis "Re" comprises a tail "e" and a head "R," symbolizing both the fundamental root of human and the head of intellect. Thus, "Re" represents the human aspect of the real physical base. On the other hand, the imaginary axis "Im" originates from imagery of an arm and water, suggesting that life emerges from water and evolves through the strength of extended arms, symbolizing the intellectual and spiritual facet of humanity.

Considering the complex number c = a + bi, the letter "c" represents a primitive sling tool—the extended arm of humans—for creation, change, and civilization. Remarkably, the real component "a" embodies the head of a sacred cow, our far root of animals, while "b" serves as a representation of birds, symbolizing the hidden spiritual essence and extended space toward the sky.

A profound coherence of existence emerges: "C = A (as Cow) + iB (as Bird)," meaning that creation is the sum of tangible real and intangible imaginary aspects of life—the total world of visible physical and unseen spiritual. Nature's complexity, beneath the surface of intricate interactions, lies in simple, shared foundational principles with coherent logic, much like how complex numbers started from pure imagination but later made real sense naturally.

> "Saint Paul said the invisible must be understood by the visible. That was not a Hebrew idea, it was Greek."
>
> –EDITH HAMILTON "MYTHOLOGY"

3. From PI to PHI

When we view the human figure of "e" - "👤", we find the extended arm of "I" reaching out upward. When we look at the lower part of the figure, we can find the form of "π" resembling the foundation of two standing legs. This idea is not entirely unfounded when tracing back the original archetype of the letter "Pi."

Semitic	Phoenician	Ancient Greek	Greek	English
⬭ ····▸	⟨ ····▸	⊤I ····▸	Π ····▸	P
Pe		Pi		

The original archetype of Pi was a mouth, which evolved into the Semitic letter Pe, and further into the Greek letter Pi and finally evolved into the English letter "P", with typical key words such as "Penis, Person and People". Notice that in the transformation from Pe to Pi, the ending letter evolved from the original human "e" to the advanced intelligent person "i," indicating the same steps from a physical person to an intelligent person.

I noticed that the ancient Greek symbol for Pi has two legs of different lengths. Interestingly, the ratio of the length of the longer right leg to the shorter left leg happens to be approximately equal to the value of Pi, which is 3.14. In many traditions, the right side is associated with female and the left side with male. This coincidence aligns with the length ratio of the X and Y chromosomes, which is also around 3.14.

$$\text{Y} \quad \text{X} \qquad \text{X} \quad \text{Y}$$
$$\Pi \dashrightarrow \quad \dashrightarrow \frac{X}{Y} = 3.14$$

"The history of π is only a small part of the history of mathematics, which itself is but a mirror of the history of man. That history is full of patterns and tendencies whose frequency and similarity are too striking to be dismissed as accidental. Like the laws of quantum mechanics, and in the final analysis, of all nature, the laws of history are evidently statistical in character. But what those laws are, nobody knows."

–PETER BECKMANN, "THE HISTORY OF π"

To conclude this chapter, I would like to introduce another symbol: "φ" (Phi), representing the golden ratio, which appears throughout nature, bringing out ultimate beauty and life's myriad mysteries. The original hieroglyph of φ was a knot of a quipu record-keeping device, which in Chinese is called "结绳记事", the early counting system. It evolved into the English letter "Q, q," leading to important keywords such as "question" and "quest": concepts of endless curiosity that drive mankind and the infinite journey of continuous discovery.

When listing these three symbols in the sequence of their alphabet (I, P, Q), I notice that I, PI, and PHI each add a new letter while retaining the same ending letter "I." The last PHI (φ) has a center letter "H," which represents sunlight "日," similar to the form of (φ), like the combination of O and I, or the number 0 and 1.

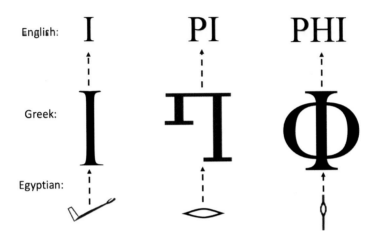

English: I   PI   PHI

Greek:

Egyptian:

The story of creation, from 0 and 1 to perfect 10, driven by the extended arm, "I", empowered by intelligence, imagination, and inspiration—is engraved in these perfect scientific symbols.

CHAPTER 5

THE COLOR OF LIFE

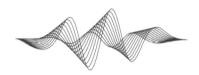

"All nature manifests itself
by means of colors to the sense of sight."

– GOETHE "THEORY OF COLORS"

In previous chapters, we observed many coincidences among words, symbols, and alphabets, uncovering common rules and patterns from archetypes of the collective unconscious that instinctively connect individual human minds. For instance, we saw how the letter "H," with its archetype of light, spans a broad world from Heaven, Hell, and Human to Head, Heart, and Hand, and from the universal elements Hydrogen and Helium to the pronouns He and Here… Life and the world cannot exist without light. In this chapter, we will explore new insights into the colors of life through the spectrum of light.

5.1 The Spectrum of Life

1. The Three Primary Colors

The first coincidental phenomena to incite my curiosity were not words, but rather coincidences arising in life from colors and the light spectrum.

I found that the three primary colors (red, yellow, and blue) seem to have an inherent connection with the three colors that have historically been used to refer to race (black, yellow, and white). The earliest people come from hot Africa and their skin has evolved a protective black sheen to stand up to the scorching red-hot sun; Asians have yellow skin corresponding to the yellow light in the middle of spectrum; and Caucasians have the lightest skin color and blue eyes that come from the shorter waves of blue light. The chronological order of the first appearance of these three races and their color characteristics coincide with the order of the three primary colors of the spectrum.

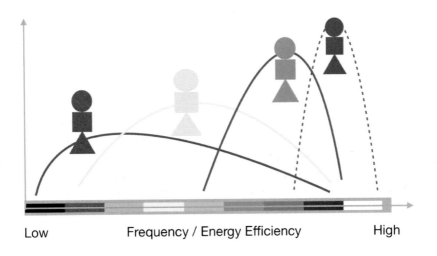

Low   Frequency / Energy Efficiency   High

In addition, the evolutionary history of the three prime ethnic groups seems to correspond to the nature of the red, yellow, and blue waves in the light spectrum. Black people evolved slowly, like long wavelength of red light, while Caucasians had the fastest evolutionary path like short-waved blue light. Asians stand in the middle with the most population, dominating the normal distribution like the middle-yellow sunlight of the visible spectrum. The last "race," the mixture of all three races, staying in front edge of evolution, corresponds to purple light, which has the shortest wavelength and highest frequency and highest peak of energy.

Furthermore, I have discovered that the evolution of the human body follows a pattern of ascending energy from bottom to top: from feet to arms, lower body to upper body, heart to head, and ultimately to spirit. Energy measures the creative force and impact any entity can produce. The human body, heart, mind, and soul are different sources of energy corresponding to what we call the Physical Quotient (PQ), Emotional Quotient (EQ), Intelligence Quotient (IQ), and Soul Quotient (SQ). They have evolved in the same pattern as sequences of waves in the light spectrum, from low to high frequency and energy.

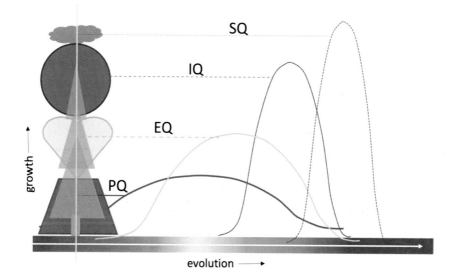

This helped me understand a life situation of my family that once confused me. My daughter, very tenanted in art and languages, often struggled with physics in primary school, and her father accused her of not being diligent. He told her: "Your father and mother were both outstanding students at Tsinghua (the top engineering university in China) and both excelled at science, you have no excuse to not excel in science." This became a big stressor to my teenager daughter who could not understand why she was not as scientifically gifted as her parents. I also struggled to understand. I discovered that this is a common phenomenon in modern families, including my bosses who were founders of great High-tech companies. As the children of great scientists evolve towards the top of their family tree, they, like my daughter, show less interest in science and engineering (solid and physical) but more talent in art and music (light and spiritual).

Inspired by the waves of light spectrum mapping with different nature of races and human body, I got the idea that life continuously evolves toward a higher energy state, in terms of growing in energy efficiency but may not in absolute total energy. For example, I can see the new generation normally eats and sleeps less yet maintain a higher energy level than their parents, similar pattern found in hummingbird. Life is inclined to live easier and with less effort, so the natural evolution is from PQ to IQ, then to SQ. The advance of evolution in life we see in younger generation is that, to reach the same level of living standard and happiness, they tend to pay less efforts than the older generation. Quite often we see at the front edge of a family tree evolution, more artistic and religious talent (SQ) shows out than scientific and engineering (IQ). Perhaps this is also the reason that religious believers normally live easier and happier lives than unbelievers.

So, should you suspect your child of not being as "smart" and hard-working as you, you may find that they are more creative and have better intuitions, and thus they can achieve a comfortable life with higher life efficiency. Overall, their life corresponds to the shorter wave of light spectrum.

2. Seven Color Spectrum

The essence of life is energy, and the primary source of energy is light. Therefore, it is natural for us to observe spectral waves within our lives. No matter how many generations humanity experiences and how large the generational gaps, the rhythm and pattern of each life has always remained consistent. It exhibits approximately seven stages, like the seven colors of the rainbow.

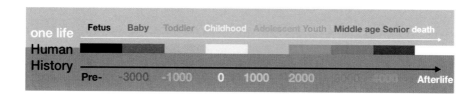

This rainbow rhythm of life is not only reflected in each individual's life, but also lies hidden in the entire life cycle of human society. If we are to compare the progression of human history with the seven stages of a person's life, it is not difficult to see that the historical waves of mankind replicate a human life on a massive scale. A brief comparison of the seven stages of human life and human history is as follows:

1. Fetal period: 0-10 months. The fetal development in the "ocean water" of the mother's body corresponds to life's early development in the ocean.

2. Infancy: 1-3 years old. Babies go from crawling to walking upright during this period. Basic language and intelligence are developed, but behaviors still mainly depend on animal instincts. Equivalent to human prehistory wherein early humans crawled upright out of the grounded animal family and started developing basic language capability…yet basically rely on their inherited animal instincts for survival.

3. Childhood: 3-6 years old, kindergarten period. Children during this period generally start to differentiate themselves and display their inherited talents, language, inspiration, imagination, and artistic talents. Corresponds to human history's period where

spoken languages emerged as did different identities of ethnic tribes, mythology, and art.

4. Childhood: 6-12 years old, elementary school stage. During this period a person's Physical Quotient will start to develop fully, and their language and communication skills mature. This is equivalent to the first historically recorded periods of civilization such as the age of oracle bones and the first Egyptian civilizations.

5. Juvenile: 12-18 years old, secondary school stage. The Emotional Quotient starts to reach maturity. This is a period of rebellion and passion, where one's talent for literature, sports, and art start reaching their peak. It corresponds to the historical period of chaotic wars, agriculture development, and the Renaissance age of art and literature.

6. Youth: 18-30 years old, the stage of higher education and independence. One's Intelligence Quotient peaks here. It is equivalent to the historical period of the Industrial Revolution and rapid developments in social systems.

7. Middle age: 30-60 years old, this is the developmental stage where one is "no more confused and knows her destiny." It's when one becomes a parent, takes on family and social responsibilities, pursues spiritual growth, and pays the most attention to the future of their offspring. It corresponds to the modern period of human history, the one we are in currently. This is the relatively stable period of human society in which countries, nations, science, religion, politics, and law are well formed and classified, and accumulate wealth for the next generation, while paying attention to Earth's environment and future while prospecting territory in space.

8. Old age: 60-90 years old, the stage where one "does as they please and return back to their roots." This is the stage when people return

to their natural instincts and experience a soul awakening. During this period, people are unable to reproduce. It is equivalent to the last wave of the current cycle of human history, where civilizations wake their primitive instincts and spirituality and start returning to the divided roots of their animal origins. At the same time, humanity will focus on restoring the earth's natural ecology and search for habitable planets in preparation to enter the next cycle.

Human society is currently in its middle-aged state and will soon enter old age. We see the world is divided and declining in many ways. Future generations will soon realize that the current disasters of 2020 such as the COVID-19 pandemic, gun violence, and crime are, like volcanoes and forest fires, aimed at restoring natural order via the law of natural selection.

3. Color Vision

Color vision is another interesting phenomenon related to the visible light spectrum. Human eyes have three color cone receptors that have the same natural frequency as the three primary colors: red, yellow, and blue lights, so we are most sensitive to the range of the visible light spectrum formed by these three colors.

Most land animals such as dogs and monkeys have only two color receptors in their eyes, so the spectrum that their eyes can differentiate is narrower than the spectrum visible to the human eye. Therefore, they are all "color blind" according to the human standard. Perhaps because of this, the natural camouflage color of these animals' coats is normally dull and lacks color. On the other hand, colorful birds and tropical fish usually have four types of color receptor cells in their eyes, allowing them to sense a wider range of the light spectrum such as ultraviolet light. Therefore, birds and fish are often more colorful. I'd imagine that to birds' eyes, humans are all color blind.

Mantis shrimp living in the deep ocean of Australia have been found to have the most color receptors in the animal kingdom—12. Although Mantis shrimp are mere inches long, they can throw the fastest punch of any animal. They strike with the force of a rifle bullet capable of shattering aquarium glass and crab shells alike. They have almost no natural enemy and sleep in the cave all day. When prey draws near, they send instant signal to their fellows to come out to catch. Mantis shrimps are also loyal to their mates throughout their life. These features, to my mind, are all signs demonstrating that Mantis shrimps are among nature's most evolved animals. All of this inspired the idea that life evolves not only from low to high light frequency but also toward a greater color vision, broadening the portion of the visible spectrum available to their eyes.

Within the range of human color vision, although most people have three color receptors, there are variations in color perception among different groups. It has been observed that Caucasians generally have more sensitive color vision than other racial groups, and color blindness is more common among men. Within the same family and environmental context, females often have better color vision than males. This is likely due to the more evolved and symmetrical nature of the XX chromosome compared to the XY chromosome.

"The eternal feminine draws us on high."

–GOETHE

To add a whimsical twist to this observation, one might imagine the range of color vision between men and women, both averaging three color receptors, as falling between the scale of two irrational constants e (2.71) and π (3.14).

Women, with their more symmetrical and perfect genes, are leading the evolution of humanity, moving us away from ground-dwelling animals toward the freedom of birds in the sky.

THE ELECTRO MAGNETIC SPECTRUM

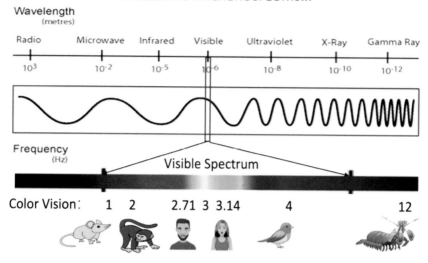

Wavelength (metres)

Radio	Microwave	Infrared	Visible	Ultraviolet	X-Ray	Gamma Ray
10^3	10^{-2}	10^{-5}	10^{-6}	10^{-8}	10^{-10}	10^{-12}

Frequency (Hz)

Visible Spectrum

Color Vision: 1   2   2.71   3   3.14   4   12

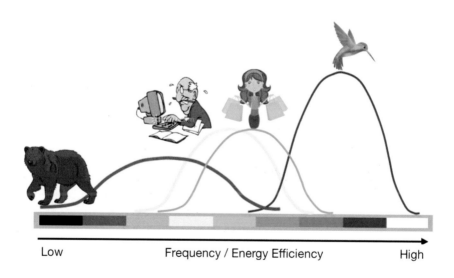

Low   Frequency / Energy Efficiency   High

The evolutionary shift toward greater color vision follows the same trend as energy efficiency. We observe that birds eat very little food but can fly to great heights in the safety of the skies. We see a similar trend as humans increase their vigor, all the while eating and sleeping less (or easily gain weight)—there is even a progressive trend towards eating vegetarian and vegan (lighter diet). This is a natural consequence of humanity moving away from primitive less efficient animals toward higher efficient ones, of following the spectrum beyond the visual wavelengths and up to the invisible spiritual plane.

4. The Yin-Yang Color Model

The Yin-Yang concept is a fundamental principle of the Yi Jing (I Ching or Book of Changes), an ancient Chinese text used for divination and philosophical guidance. Yin and Yang represent the dualistic nature of the universe, where Yin is associated with qualities such as female, the moon, night, darkness, coldness, passivity, and receptivity, while Yang is linked to male, light, day, brightness, warmth, activity, and creativity. These opposing forces are interconnected and interdependent, constantly interacting and transforming into one another to maintain balance and harmony in the cosmos. Yi Jing uses this dynamic interplay of Yin and Yang to interpret changes and provide insights into various aspects of life, emphasizing the importance of balance and the cyclical nature of existence.

Like life, colors can be classified by temperatures: so-called warm and cool colors. Red, orange, and yellow are considered warm colors —Yang, while green, blue, and purple are considered cool colors—Yin. Yin, the cool colors of a feminine nature have higher frequency and energy than the warmer, masculine Yang colors, such as blue flame vs red flame. This is consistent with our conclusions about color vision. Black and white, the pair of ultimate extremes, are the "Taiji" colors: black is extremely Yin whereas white is extremely Yang. But no true black or white can ever truly exist. By the Yin-Yang principle, Yin in its extremity turns to Yang, while an extreme instance of Yang will turn to Yin.

The three primary colors mentioned earlier—red, yellow, and blue—are based on the traditional color models that come from mixing dyes. A more modern color model is based on the colors of light that you see represented in your monitor's pixels, where the three primary colors that make up the spectrum are red, green and blue. These two color models coexist for different applications: the traditional model, shown on the left is often used for painting and mixing dyes, while the modern model shown to right is used for screens and mixing lights. There are slight differences in these two models that still cannot not explained or understood.

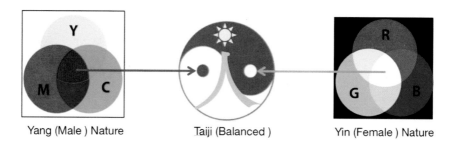

Yang (Male) Nature   Taiji (Balanced)   Yin (Female) Nature

Take note the core color of each set—the overlapping mixture of all its colors—which becomes black in the traditional dye model and white in the modern light model. As dye are particles, which are heavier than light waves, I will call the traditional dye model the "male model" and the modern light model the "female model". This is similar to men who appear Yang-masculine from outside but deep inside their core are Yin-feminine, and women are generally stronger and more positive (Yang) inside than men are but appear feminine on the outside. This Yin-Yang nature is best illustrated by the *Taiji*'s pair of white (Yang-male) and black (Yin-female) fish. The two models of color with their opposite cores is echoed precisely by the two halves of the Taiji model with the diametrically opposing eyes.

The coincidences found within color models are yet another demonstration of the consistency between Yin-Yang's logic, color theory, and the natural laws. Just like Goethe said in his Theory of Colors: "All the natural phenomena we observe can be expressed through colors."

5.2 The Color of Flags

The Chinese word for flag "旗帜" is pronounced the same as the word for temperament "气质", which is the collective unconscious message indicating that each nationality's temperament is represented in their flag, as was the case of the tribal flags of antiquity. Colors manifest life's nature, and you will find the colors on flags to be like words: not the creation of a mere individual designer, but the result of the collective unconscious's instincts following natural law and the spectral order, i.e., the Yin-Yang principles.

The fundamental nature of humanity is a mix between male and female roots. Countless generations of male and female genes stirred together have caused the male and female temperaments to co-mingle as well. For instance, there is a well-marked trend in modern society towards more genderless and homosexual people. Despite this, the fundamental differences between men and women still exist. Natural selection creates three distinct groups with different strengths: hyperfeminine, hypermasculine, and neutrals. This is the same reason that most societies are naturally divided into three groups: left wing, right wing, and the moderates. Fundamental political differences and distinct worldviews are rooted in the difference between female and male nature of humanity, or precisely between Yin and Yang. In the same way that these divided roots are embodied in an individual's psychological characteristics, they are also reflected in the colors of national flags and emblem and the logos of organizations.

Take as example the comparison of two flags representing two extreme groups of people: the South African flag on the left, representing the origins of humanity and the pride flag on the right displayed by the LGBTQ community, represent the modern or final group of humanity with the evenly spread rainbow colors.

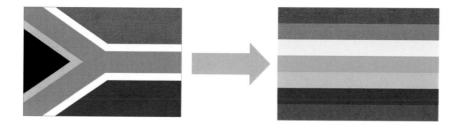

The South African flag is composed of six colors including the extreme Yin and Yang of black and white, along with the four prime colors: red, yellow, green, and blue. They are displayed symmetrically with the green tree of life—the Y gene, in the center. The tree grows from left to right, starting from the extreme Yin of a black delta, which passes through the yellow light of the sun on toward the outer white light. The Yang (male) red fire or volcano mountain rests atop the Y, while the Yin (female) blue water or ocean lies to the bottom. Could you think of a better image than this potent combination of colors, rife with meaning, to illustrate the key elements and their relationship to the origin of life?

Likewise, the pride flag is composed of six colors. The main difference being that the extreme black and white colors have disappeared and now the pattern is an evenly lined rainbow. The bottom line is purple—a mixture of red and blue, which does not appear in the South African flag, representing this mixed-blood group. It represents the balanced "neutral" people who mix evenly the masculine with the feminine. Like the flowers and fruits on the pinnacle of each family tree, they are generally more spiritual and, like the birds, evolving away from the ground animals to pursue ease and harmony of life.

Like words, the evolution of the colors and patterns of flags and logos instinctively follow the order prescribed by the light spectrum, starting from the extreme Yin of black and Yang of Red, shifts to yellows and greens in the middle, then moves on toward the Yin of Blue, and lastly turns to the extreme Yang of white. The colors match the temperaments or souls of the life spirits that they represent.

I will now present several flag color patterns of countries who are geographically proximate yet have very different national characteristics, and how they can be identified through the colors of their flags. You will see the colors of Yin and Yang reflected in their national temperaments.

Let's first look at a pair of Asian countries which historically haven't gotten along: Japan and South Korea: Their flags share the same background: white, which represents islands, the extreme Yang(male nature of environment). The Japanese flag is adorned with a red sun (Yang) in its center, reflecting its extreme Yang (masculine) temperament. The Yang characteristics are borne out in a typical stereotype of Japan: aggressive, warmongering, persistent, fond of tools, cars, and technology. Opposite, the South Korean flag has the image of the Taiji in its center composed of red (Yang) and blue (Yin), reflecting the balanced feminine core of their temperament, and again borne out by the typical stereotype of Korea: religious, and good at movies, beauty, and small commodities —all typical female natures of humanity. As two extreme nations of Asia, they are as distinct as the divided male-female roots of a person "人".

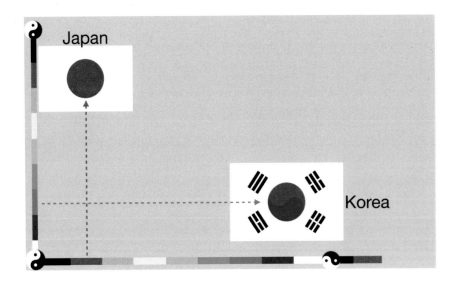

Europe has a similar pair of Yin-Yang neighboring countries who are geographically adjacent yet have very different temperaments: France and Germany. When the colors and patterns of their flags are compared with knowledge of the light spectrum, the Yin and Yang roots of their ethnic differences are immediately revealed:

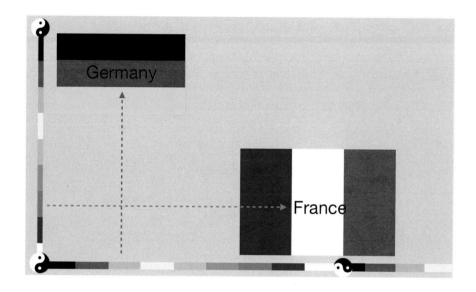

Both flags are composed of three stripes of color, the most obvious difference being that the stripes are aligned horizontally (Yin-female nature) in the French flag and vertically (Yang-male nature) in the German flag. This indicates that the major differences between the French and German can be likened to the differences between woman and man.

The sequence of colors in the French flag goes from the blue (Yin-female) in the left toward red (Yang-male) to the right, with the core consisting of the extreme Yang of white. This reflects the classical dynamics of a woman's nature evolving from pure female genes toward male traits.

The sequence of colors found in the German flag go from yellow (mildly Yang) at the bottom, through red in the core (very Yang) and on toward the black (extreme Yin) at the top. This illustrates male nature evolving from the original male gene to an extremely masculine center before finally returning to the extreme Yin—its grandmotherly origin—at its core.

Not unlike the Japanese, the Germans display typical masculine characteristics: they are disciplined, hardworking, good at tools, cars, and war. The French, on the other hand, are similar to Korea in being famous for pretty women, perfume, fashion, movies, food, and leisure.

Let's look at another example of three nations in Northern Europe: Norway, Sweden, and Finland:

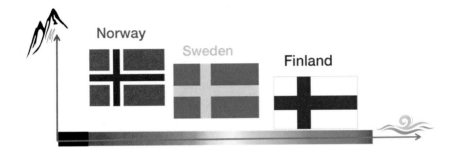

Many European countries' national flags feature a cross pattern, which originates from the flag of the ancient Roman Empire's crusaders. The earliest and most famous amongst these is St. George's Cross, consisting of a red cross on a white background. The flags of the three neighboring Northern European countries Norway, Sweden, and Finland all have the same St. George's cross pattern, but evolved into cooler color yellow and blue comparing to the original red cross. I displayed these three flags on the same spectrum. If you're familiar with the cultural differences between these three nations, you will see their key differences reflected in the contrasting colors, where the background represents the geography and environment and the cross represents the core Yin-Yang nature of its nationals.

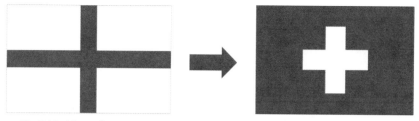

The Original Cross of Saint Gorge   The Final White Cross of Switzerland

Now let's compare two extreme variations of cross flags: the original Crusader flag, as shown on Saint George, and the current flag of Switzerland, where the United Nations headquarters is located. We observe that the cross and background colors are reversed, symbolizing a new evolutionary life cycle of these fatherlands from their origins in the Roman Empire.

Next, let us move on to the Americas and compare Canada, Mexico, and the United States. With Yang colors of white and red in common America coastline environments, the major difference between these three countries can be seen in the identifying colors of red, green, and blue in sequence.

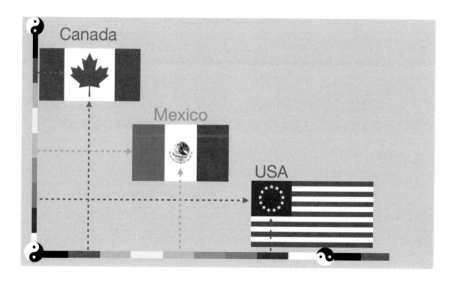

Northernmost Canada is represented by a red maple leaf symbolizing the Yang nature at the core of their temperament. Traditionally, Canadians share the northern characteristics of being manly, tall, upright, and straightforward. Contrast this with the more southerly Mexico's characteristic colors, which begin with green (Yin-female) on the left, end with red (Yang-male) to the right, with an image at the core: a brown eagle representing their native origin and bond with nature. The United States is located between Canada and Mexico. Its original flag bore the core image of a circle of white (extreme Yang) stars within a deep blue (Yin) ocean, representing the mixed blood and cultures of its many immigrants. Their combined stars emerged from the deep blue ocean and evolved the fastest and with the greatest efficiency, thereby becoming the leader of the modern world.

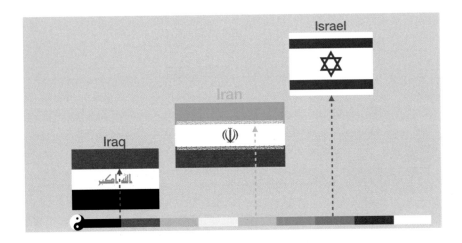

The same pattern of three prime color sequences is also found in three Middle Eastern countries, which may help to make sense of the unreasonable troubles of this land with contrasting nature of the red (male) Iraq and the blue (female) Israel. The above examples should start to give a sense that the conflicts and contradictions between human ethnicities and nationalities are deeply rooted within the differences of two opposing ancestral lines. They are just as brothers and sisters who seem alike when they are young yet turn out differently when they grow up, due to the different blood lines that they have inherited through their mother and father.

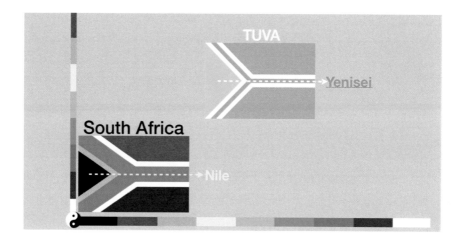

Finally, l present my favorite contrast of two flags: the South African flag and the flag of Tuva, a state in the Russian Federation. They have the same pattern of a tree root or the Y gene. The difference lies in the colors. The Y of South Africa is green, originating from the black delta representing a cradle of life, Okavango. The Tuvan Y is blue, originating from the yellow triangle representing the Gobi Desert, a 2nd origin of life in Asia and thus corresponding to the yellow color of sunlight. The front edge of the origin triangles displays another contrast: the one in South Africa yellow light, whereas Tuva's is white. The emigration from African to Asia went through the older warmer Nile River, while the emigration from Asian to Europe went through the younger cooler Yenisei river.

The pattern and colors of flags conceal many secrets. Careful observation will display how the patterns and colors of flags come from the collective unconscious and display a history of life's evolution. Fragments of knowledge splintered from individual consciousness are absorbed back into the whole organic universe of the collective unconsciousness. As Carl Jung predicted: once the collective unconscious becomes conscious, it will lead to fast expansion of knowledge.

5.3 Colors of Logos

Logos are the soul of any commercial entity or product brand. They represent the founder's vision and dream in the same way that a name represents a person or a flag a country. By now, you should not find it surprising that logo colors evolve instinctively with the history of the business or product instead of relying on an individual designer. The same as the colors of life, logo colors evolve from black to white, heavy to light, low frequency to high frequency, real to virtual, and from low energy to high energy —the order of colors in the light spectrum.

As each national flag has gone through many years of strife, change, and challengers, they are extreme symbols and so it is easy to find their pattern within the universal collective unconscious. But there are countless logos over a broad scope, so absent big data techniques, it is more difficult to pick out the patterns that they conform to. In the same way as we focus on a few key words and most frequently used alphabets, we will focus on a few extreme examples presented by large companies that have had a great impact on their industries (refer to rationales about this approach in Chapter 9).

I observed in the fields that I am familiar, the logos of many innovative and revolutionary businesses started with black and red, and when reaching the mature stage, evolved into a mostly white and purple palette.

The Above example is from IT industry that I worked with, comparing the logo's evolution through three stages (start, growth, and maturity) in the three giants of the IT industry: IBM, Microsoft, and Apple. You can see the clear trend in the evolution of the logo's color from a heavier black through rainbow colors and finally towards a lighter white.

In my last few years of work at IBM, I oversaw PLM business while working with IBM's industrial solutions partner Dassault System (DS), the globally leading brand in computer-aided design (CAD). After I noticed that the colors in DS's logo had changed from dark blue to a more balanced mixture of the three prime colors, I shared my observation about the patterns exhibited by logos' colors with DS's founder, Francis Bernard. Immediately, he sent me an email with a rarely-known logo he had designed when he first founded DS…. the logo was pure black!

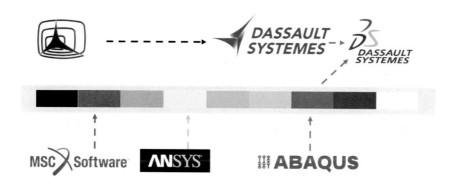

I have displayed DS's logo's evolution in the figure above. On the second line, I placed the logos of the three leading companies in the CAE (Computer Aided Engineering) field in order of their creation. I worked four years in this high-tech segment after I left IBM. The first company, MSC, has a pure red logo, the 2nd, ANSYS, is marked by its unique yellow color, and the 3rd one, ABAQUS, is all blue. Just as most of top three players in an industry will normally develop, so too do the theme colors of their logos reflecting the competitive strength from the traditional solid origin toward newer and leaner organization with increasingly energy efficiency.

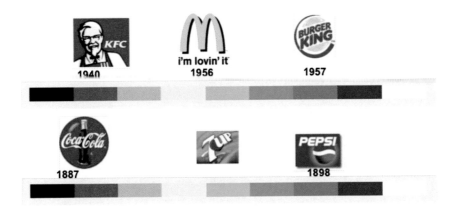

Take another example from the fast food industry that we are all familiar with: the first player, KFC's, logo is back and red, the 2nd player, McDonalds, is yellow, and the 3rd player, Burger King, adds a mix of blue and red, i.e., purple. A similar sequence of colors is found in the three leading brands of soda drinks: Coca-Cola, 7-up, and Pepsi.

Let's look at the automobile industry, which most people are acquainted with. Each major brand has gone through quite a few models, each accompanied by a change of logo. Nowadays, we see many cars sporting silver and white colors, just as black cars were more popular in the old times and white cars have more popularity in modern days. The evolution of car logos contains the same universal pattern, proceeding from black and red at the beginning to silver and white at the end, in between passing in sequence through the stages of life's colors.

Not unlike Japan's national flag, the logos of Japanese cars like Toyota and Honda all started in red. Honda has since changed its logo to entirely silver, whereas Toyota kept their name in red letter and changed the image into silver, keeping its male identity and remaining the No. 1 "male" car maker, known for Jeeps and SUVs.

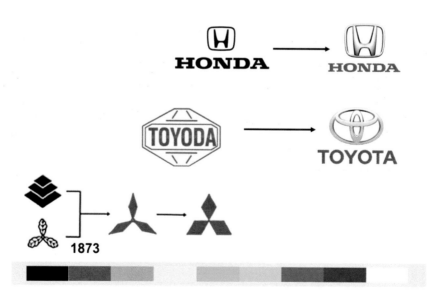

"When we are attracted by some extraordinary phenomena, it will first arouse our curiosity. In order to continue this curiosity, we will have an interest in exploration, and then gradually become familiar with the objects we are curious about. In this observation in the process, we will have various opinions that differ from person to person at the beginning. Later, we will be forced to disagree, differentiate, and then merge, until we finally present something that more or less satisfies more people."

—GOETHE, COLOR THEORY

Goethe, using instinct and natural observation, challenged the physical theories of color put forth by Newton, the eminent scientific authority of his time. Goethe believed that colors are not dictated by the laws of physics alone, but also have a chemical and physiological nature, and he emphasized the influence of the senses on color perception. Although his poetic style and elegant yet subjective arguments caused *Color Theory to be* regarded as a "physics novel", his keen observations and intuitions inspired future generations as much as Newton's scientific theories.

I hope that by exploring the color patterns emanating from the collective unconscious that we discussed in this chapter will pique the reader's curiosity in colors and broaden their mind and vision. Remember that to the bird's eye, humans are all color blind. Once we acknowledge that the visible light spectrum is but a small section in the broader spectrum, it should not be too difficult to imagine that the world humans perceive is but a pinpoint of existence within an infinite universe. What was nonsense today may make sense in future.

CHAPTER 6

THE PAREIDOLIA ROCKS

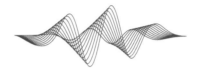

After familiarizing myself with the original meanings of each letter, I began to notice endless coincidences in words, names, logos, and symbols, revealing a common thread across different times, spaces, and cultures. This practice became a habit, and soon, meaningful coincidences would catch my eye unbidden whenever I encountered something interesting.

Three years ago, I moved from California to Prescott in Arizona. On my first day driving into the town passing the Granite Dells area, I was captivated by the granite boulders along the highway, which looked like piles of ancient monsters. Since then, I developed a new hobby: taking pictures of rocks with human or ghost-like faces during my hikes. My phone quickly filled up with these kinds of photos. I began to wonder why I always saw these ghostly rock heads. Then, the coincidences of words came to mind: the Chinese word "石头" for rock literally means "rock head," and the English word "rock" has the head-letter "r," which

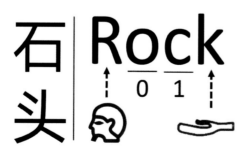

represents a human head in Egyptian hieroglyphs, and the tail-letter "k," which resembles a human hand. Between the head and hand sits "OC," the magic "0,1" signifying the core nature of origin and change. It seems that some key elements of human evolution were marked within the rock record.

As I started to believe in the wisdom embedded in the archetypes of words, these coincidences made me think seriously about why I often found rocks resembling human heads. Just as with words, the chances of finding human heads among rocks are not equal; it happens most often in ancient geological sites like Prescott's Granite Dells, which have geological histories over a billion years old, embodying "primitive" archetypes. This led me to add a new word to my vocabulary: "pareidolia," which intriguingly resembles the word "nonsense" and thus opened up another new world beyond common sense.

6.1 The Pareidolia View

Pareidolia, according to definition on Wikipedia is a psychological phenomenon of easily seeing human faces. In Chinese, it is translated as "空想性错视," meaning "imaginative misperception." The formal explanation is that the brain assigns actual meaning to external stimuli, but this meaning is purely coincidental and does not truly exist. When I see this definition, I can understand what it means in common sense. However, I feel it is somewhat biased due to our normal tendency to deny things we cannot sense their exists. The word "pareidolia" is derived from two Greek words: This first from "para" meaning "beside, alongside" and the 2nd from "eidolon" meaning "image, form". This is the same etymology of the word "nonsense" which is combined by "non" and "sense" that simply means "things we cannot sense", that may not be all nonsenses. Thus, none judgmentally, the original meaning of pareidolia should be understood as "something beside the image", which may contain deeper meanings beyond what we judge "none" by conventional perceptions. Therefore, I believe translating "pareidolia" into Chinese as "幻视—imaginative perception" instead of "Imaginative misperception" is more objective.

In fact, pareidolia is not a rare phenomenon in human history. Many artists during the Renaissance, such as Andrea Mantegna, the fresco artist of the Italian church ceiling, Leonardo da Vinci, and Vincent van Gogh, created timeless masterpieces through pareidolia. For instance, Andrea Mantegna's ceiling frescoes are a brilliant example of this phenomenon. Modern science has also applied the principles of pareidolia to image recognition technology, especially in complex artificial intelligence neural networks. Research has shown that one mechanism of pareidolia is the human eye's innate sensitivity to facial features, enabling quicker recognition of human faces while obscuring other lifeless details in the image. Studies on pareidolia have found that this phenomenon is more common among children than adults because it is a primitive instinct, and children rely more on these instincts than adults do.

A common form of pareidolia in daily life is seeing various animals and human shapes in clouds and satellite images. A typical example is a photograph of the Martian surface taken by NASA's rover, which featured a striking human face, sparking widespread curiosity. (Image source: Wikipedia)

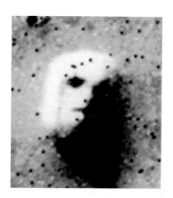

In fact, the images of cosmic nebulae often convey a more vivid and enchanting sense of the earthly world than clouds in the sky. Many nebulae are named with a romantic flair reminiscent of pareidolia. For instance, the reflection nebula IC 2118, located about 1000 light-years away in the vicinity of Orion, is also known as the "Witch Head Nebula." The name comes from the unmistakable profile of a witch's head visible in the nebula's image. (Image source: Wikipedia)

Since pareidolia is a human instinct, it can be better understood by understanding Carl Jung's *Collective Unconscious* and the *Archetype* which is basically about the primitive instincts beyond individual senses. We see more pareidolia images in nebulae and rocks from ancient geological sites because they are closer to the ultimate archetypes of life's origin.

"In addition to our immediate consciousness, which is of a thoroughly personal nature and which we believe to be the only empirical psyche, there exists a second psychic system of a collective, universal, and impersonal nature which is identical in all individuals. This collective unconscious does not develop individually but is inherited. It consists of pre-existent forms, the archetypes, which can only become conscious secondarily and which give definite form to certain psychic contents...the collective unconscious is anything but an incapsulated personal system; it is sheer objectivity, as wide as the world and open to all the world"

—CARL JUNG

6.2 The Granite Ghosts in Prescott

Prescott, though not widely known, was the former capital city of Arizona before Phoenix. It emerges as an oasis in the midst of the desert, blessed with abundant sunshine and a pleasantly cool climate. In the summer of 2020, my husband and I moved here from the Bay Area of California and instantly fell in love with this town because it is a true paradise for outdoor lovers like us. For the first time in my life, I encountered so many geological wonders.

The Granite Dells of Prescott is a striking geological formation characterized by massive, rounded granite boulders and rugged terrain. These granite rocks were formed approximately 1.4 billion years ago during the Precambrian era, a period marked by significant volcanic activity and the slow cooling of magma deep beneath the Earth's surface. Over time, the granite was exposed through uplift and erosion, creating the unique landscape seen today.

I am astonished every time I hike around Watson Lake in the Granite Dells area. The piles of rocks around the lake vividly resemble human skeletons, crowded together like penguins, reminding me of the biblical flood story that once wiped out humanity.

As ancient as they are, these rocks reveal geological archetypes of human figures, similar to how the words "石头" (rock head), "rock," and "river" all contain the "human head" in their roots. This mirrors the scenario described in Greek mythology: "Before there were gods, heaven and earth had been formed. They were the first parents. The Titans were their children, and the gods were their grandchildren." These ancient rocks, as old as one-third of Earth's age, are the remains of the Titans once roaming the Earth.

Here are some examples of rock heads from Watson Lake. Almost every step of my hikes in this area leads me to encounter scattered heads like these. One of the most astonishing finds is a rock resembling a giant hand. It reminds me of a remarkable dinosaur footprint I saw at the Dinosaur Discovery Museum in St. George, as shown below.

Prescott Watson Lake

Dinosaur Discovery Museum, Saint George

By modern geological classification, the giant hand is an ordinary granite rock, incomparable to the precious dinosaur bone fossils. However, I cannot help but think of them together. The dinosaur footprints are only about 200 million years old, while the hand-shaped granite rock is over a billion years old. Imagine that if the dinosaur bone fossil were to remain buried for over a billion years, it might transform into what scientists today classify as a seemingly insignificant rock.

Fossils are typically formed from the remains of plants and animals that undergo long-term chemical processes underground. During this transformation, organic material is gradually replaced or filled in by minerals, eventually forming fossils. Fossils are preserved within geological layers and can last for millions of years.

Although scientifically defined fossils differ from ordinary rocks in composition, both are primarily composed of minerals such as quartz (silicon dioxide) and calcite (calcium carbonate). Calcite, also found in bones, makes them as hard as or even harder than rocks. After prolonged erosion by wind and water, the hard calcium carbonates in bones become exposed, making rocks appear like the skeletons of animals and humans. This process is similar to the formation of fossils but takes much longer. Over time, the traces of organic material fully mineralize and disappear, leaving behind what scientists classify as rock.

There is another explanation for why rocks often take the shape of humans. In ancient China, people believed that the soul comprised a duality known as "hun" (魂) and "po" (魄). "Hun" represents the yang or spiritual aspect, while "po" represents the yin or physical aspect. At the beginning of life, hun and po are unified within the living being. After death, hun ascends to the clouds in the sky, whereas po descends with the body into the earth.

Similar to many ancient myths and beliefs, this concept of hun and po has been passed down orally among the people and is immortalized in the collective unconscious through written characters. The Chinese character for "hun" (魂) consists of "cloud" (云) and "ghost" (鬼), while the character for "po" (魄) comprises "white" (白) and "ghost" (鬼), signifying a visible physical ghost. The concept of

white + ghost ----→ 魄 po

the yin-yang soul is documented in classic texts such as the master dictionary "Shuowen Jiezi (说文解字)." One statement from "Zuo Zhuan," one of the most famous historical texts, says, "The essence of the heart is called the soul. Without the soul, how can one survive?"

This ancient belief tells us that the soul not only exists but is also perceivable. It resides beyond our ordinary consciousness, hidden in what is called the collective unconscious. In common terms, this is generally known as "fate," which governs our lives. We may not understand it fully, but no one denies existence of soul. The awareness of the Yin-Soul (魄 po) residing inside the rocks, make me understand that the pareidolia view of rocks is not pure illusion, but indeed as the original word defined: seeing things beyond the images -the immortal souls of mortal human.

6.3 The Mystique of Sedona

The famous town of Sedona in northern Arizona, near the Grand Canyon, is surrounded by stunning red rock canyons. The spectacular natural landscape often makes me feel a deeper connection with nature and the universe. Sedona has become an increasingly popular tourist destination, not just for its natural beauty but also because it has become a center of the New Age spiritual movement. This has drawn many people interested in spirituality, energy healing, and the supernatural. Many believe that Sedona's unique geographic and geological features generate special energies, referred to as "vortex energies" or "magnetic fields," which are thought to promote physical, mental, and spiritual balance and healing. Although there is no scientific evidence to support these claims, the large and growing community based on supernatural beliefs and spiritual practices suggests something meaningful and profound.

Living nearby, I frequently visit Sedona. I've hiked many of its trails multiple times, and each time, the experience of being surrounded by the various forms of red rock feels fresh and mysterious. This sense of mystery intensified after I became aware of the souls in rocks. The landscape seemed filled with "spirit rocks" everywhere I looked.

One of my most memorable hikes is along the West Fork of Oak Creek Trail, which follows a tributary of the Colorado River. The rock cliffs along the water's edge are filled with enigmatic shapes, making me feel as if I were in a prehistoric world, with spirits and deities within arm's reach. At the trail's end, the creek makes a large bend, and crossing the water, I was struck by the sight of a massive boulder that looked uncannily like a grand Buddha statue, with the sun creating a halo around its head. Next to it was another rock resembling a fierce-looking Luohan, or Arhat, so lifelike and awe-inspiring.

This experience helped me understand why Sedona is considered a center of supernatural energy. The area is filled with vibrant spirits of ancient rocks. Six million years ago, the Colorado River carved out the Grand Canyon, and countless storms and floods have since exposed the remains of these prehistoric earth giants. These ancient bones, or the "po-魄", carrying the eternal soul and spirit of the ancestors, continue to nourish their long-forgotten descendants. When people meditate here, they feel the energy fields because, in the absence of noise and distractions, their minds resonate with the sacred souls of these divine rocks.

With this newfound awareness, I began to notice that many of Sedona's trail names are inspired by the distinctive shapes of the rocks they lead to. Popular hiking trails such as "Cathedral Rock Trail," "Devil's Bridge Trail," "Soldier Pass Trail," and "Seven Sacred Pools Trail" are named after these iconic rock formations. While walking on the Soldier Pass Trail, I noticed clusters of massive red rocks resembling arrays of dignified generals and soldiers.

Another unforgettable sight in Sedona is a Catholic chapel built on a rocky hill, backed by red cliffs and facing a vast canyon. The chapel's glass walls reflect a statue of the crucified Jesus, seemingly embraced by the Grand Canyon and bathed in sunlight. Though I am not religious, I am instinctively drawn to this chapel. The surrounding cliffs resemble intricately carved rock statues, filled with expressive and vivid human faces. Near the entrance, I saw a massive rock that perfectly resembled a solemn statue of a saint.

Historically, Sedona was one of the earliest settlements of the Navajo and Apache tribes in the southwestern United States, with their history dating back to around 1500 BCE. The Navajo have many myths about creation, heroes, animals, and nature. They worship the Earth Mother, believing the earth to be one of the deities that created the world. The Apache tradition is rich in myths and stories explaining their views on nature, spirits, and human origins. Sacred names from ancient legends have been carried into modern names of this area. The name of Yavapai County, for example, is derived from a sacred goddess in Apache lore, considered the mother of all things and associated with life, fertility, and the balance of nature and society.

The mystique of Sedona is not magic. The choice of a site for worship, the ancient beliefs in immortal human gods, and the New Age supernatural feelings did not come from nowhere. They are all revelations of the immortal souls of humans, the "魂魄" (hun and po), living inside these ancient rocks that formed the archetypes of collective unconscious.

6.4 The Creator of Crater

Located near Flagstaff, Arizona, Meteor Crater is one of Earth's best-preserved impact craters. It was formed over 50,000 years ago when a massive iron-nickel meteorite, approximately 150 feet wide and weighing hundreds of thousands of tons, struck the outskirts of Flagstaff. In 2022, during my first visit to this crater, I watched the educational film "Impact" at the museum. The film profoundly impacted me and sparked a strong interest in meteorites. The image on the right captures the moment of a rapidly descending black meteorite impacting Earth, resembling a vivid giant black human head.

After watching the film, I often thought of Chinese words such as "源头" (origin), "猿头" (ape head), and "圆头" (round head) due to their phonetic similarities. Another intriguing phonetic coincidence is between the words "crater" and "creator," both carrying the tail-letter "r," which symbolizes the human head in Egyptian hieroglyphs. This coincidence suggests to me that the far origin of human heads may come from the crater, hinting that meteorites from outer space could be connected to the creation of life on Earth.

Meter Crater in Flagstaff   The Documentary "Impact"

We know that life on Earth originated in the oceans. In fact, water is a prerequisite for the emergence of life on any planet. Scientific research suggests that a significant portion of Earth's water may have come from extraterrestrial sources, including meteorites. In addition to water, scientific research has found that meteorites contain organic compounds and key precursors to life. For example, the Murchison meteorite, which fell in Australia in 1969, is one of the most studied meteorites. It contains a variety of organic compounds, including amino acids essential for life. This discovery supports the idea that such compounds may have played a role in the origin of life on Earth. Certain types of meteorites, known as carbonaceous chondrites, are rich in organic material, including amino acids and water. These primitive meteorites, originating from the asteroid belt, preserve and reflect the initial conditions of the early solar system.

Asteroids are rocky and metallic bodies in the solar system. By examining the composition of these bodies, particularly those containing water and organic molecules, scientists can trace the chemical evolution of the solar system and explore the possibility of life originating within it. The asteroid belt is considered a potential location where life might exist in the solar system.

The asteroid Bennu is the largest and most carbon-rich asteroid sample returned to Earth to date. Bennu's history dates back 4.5 billion years, and its material composition is closely linked to the early conditions of the solar system. This is not only a tremendous scientific achievement but also provides valuable insights into the cosmic origins of life on Earth. Some scientists have long proposed that Earth was struck by water-bearing asteroids, making it a habitable planet. The dust samples from Bennu support this hypothesis, offering evidence that these asteroid impacts brought the essential elements for life to Earth.

The name "Bennu" for the asteroid sample comes from an ancient Egyptian mythological bird that is often associated with the sun, creation, and rebirth. The Bennu bird is linked to the Egyptian god Osiris and is considered a symbol of renewal and the passage of time.

The name was selected through a public naming contest organized by the Planetary Society and NASA in 2013. The winning entry was submitted by a third-grade student, who suggested the name because the spacecraft's arm and solar panels resembled the outstretched wings of the Bennu bird. This symbolic connection made "Bennu" a fitting name for the mission, which aims to study the origins of the solar system and bring back a sample from the asteroid.

Additionally, I discovered a fascinating coincidence about the name "Bennu." It combines the "Benben Stone," a sacred object in Egyptian creation myth, with the river "Nu," from which the Benben Stone is said to have emerged.

Despite the diverse myths from different periods and regions of ancient Egypt, there are common threads among them. Firstly, they all believe that the world emerged from a boundless, primordial watery chaos known as "Nu." Secondly, they hold that the first thing to emerge from this primordial water was a pyramid-shaped mound called the "Benben Stone," also referred to as the Sun Stone, Pyramid Stone, or Stone of Destiny.

The Egyptians believed the Benben Stone was a mysterious mound that emerged from the primordial waters at the beginning of creation, symbolizing the origin of life and order. The creator sun god Ra (also known as Atum) settled upon it. In Heliopolis, the Benben Stone was a sacred stone in the temple, where the first rays of sunlight were believed to shine. They worshipped the bird god Bennu, also known as the Phoenix, which nested on the Benben Stone, representing the soul of the sun god Ra (Atum).

As a symbol of the origin of the world and life, the Benben Stone became the prototype for the capstones of the Great Pyramids and obelisks, making it a central element of Egyptian religion and culture.

I came across a paper titled "Investigation on the Origins of the Benben Stone - Was it an Iron Meteorite?" by Robert G. Bauval on his website. Bauval suggests that considering the deceased pharaoh's stellar destiny and the textual references to his "iron bones," the cosmic origin of the Benben Stone, and its conical shape, it is reasonable to speculate that this sacred stone was originally a "directed iron meteorite." A well-preserved conical iron meteorite displayed in Mexico City looks like a pyramid capstone. Bauval cites historical examples of human meteorite worship, including the revered Black Stone in the Kaaba at Mecca, which geologists believe is an ancient meteorite. He also quotes passages from the Pyramid Texts, stating, "The king's bones are iron, the king's members are immortal stars," inferring that the pyramid's Benben Stone symbolizes not only the sun god but also the star-souls of the kings, eternally reborn between heaven and earth, perpetuating life.

Up to now, with all these interconnections between myth and science, beliefs and reason, observation and imagination, I hope you can see how "Imagination encircles the world."

I'd like to conclude this chapter with another word coincidence: the word "star," like "crater" and "creator," also carries the tail-letter "r," symbolizing the human head. In Chinese, the word for star, "星," consists of the character for "sun" (日) above the character for "life" (生). The ancient oracle bone script for "star" vividly illustrates the connection between stars, stones, and life growing out of them. The head-letter of "star," the same as that of "stone" and "seed," is "s," originally symbolizing a tooth. It is the hardest part of the human body, and when "planted" or buried underground, it can last millions of years, becoming the earliest evidence of life we have found in human history.

CHAPTER 7

THE PAREIDOLIA EARTH

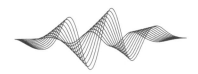

"The Greeks did not believe that the gods created the universe. It was the other way about: the universe created the gods. Before there were gods heaven and earth had been formed. They were the first parents. The Titans were their children, and the gods were their grandchildren."

—MYTHOLOGY, EDITH HAMILTON

Among all the coincidences I have discovered, the most fascinating is the pareidolia observed in satellite images from Google Earth. These images become a source of archetypes, connecting geographic formations with ancient mythologies. I am astonished to find the most vivid images of Titans and the souls of human on Earth.

In this chapter, I will guide you through the mysteries perceived through pareidolia, much like the word "nonsense," which may not be just a coincidental view without meaning. Instead, these perceptions are another set of secret messengers from the collective unconscious, often unrecognized or ignored by our normal senses.

7.1 The Ancestors from Africa

In the summer of 2015, my sister and I drove to my hometown of Penglai, located in Shandong, China. As she drove, I glanced at the map of the Shandong Peninsula and was amazed to discover a satellite view resembling a giant roaring tiger, leaping towards the east.

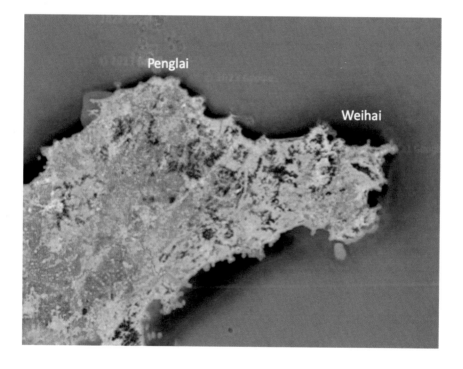

This intrigued me since Shandong is the home of the famous legend of "Wu-Song Beats Tiger". In addition, the northeast China, situated right across the ocean above the giant tiger, is now the home to the largest wild tiger reserve in the country. What a coincidence!

From this, I developed a hobby of browsing Google Earth images wherever I go and whenever I come across an interesting site. Over time, many random screen captures became connected, merging great legendary figures and historical stories into a vivid graphic book of the unknown human prehistory on Earth.

1. The Lion Kingdom

When you rotate the Google map 90 degrees from the standard view, you'll uncover a stunning image: a giant Lion of Africa (on the left) facing a pair of human figures (on the right). The upper figure resembles a man from Western Europe, with Spain and Portugal forming his head, while the lower figure depicts a woman from the Middle East, with Turkey as her head. This image resembles the archetypal scene from the modern film "The Lion King," where Mufasa, the father, whose nose points to Simba's, imparts lessons to the young future king and his girlfriend.

2. The Motherland of Southern Africa

Grandma Mt. Eve: While the contours of the African coastline form the shape of a giant lion, the lion's tail in the south resembles a perfect woman's head facing southwest. I call this formation "Grandma Mt. Eve." "Mt" stands for both "Mountain" and "Mitochondrial," symbolizing the unbroken common matrilineal ancestor of humanity. In the image, as well as in the following images, I have highlighted the details with a screen pencil to make the faces I saw easier for others to recognize. You can explore and find this vivid figure yourself on Google Earth. Pay attention to two important locations on Eve's head: First on her temple, there is a mark which looks like the root of a tree, it is Okavango Delta. Then at her jaw, you can find another face facing the west at the bottom tip of southern Africa. Following is the enlarged images of these spots:

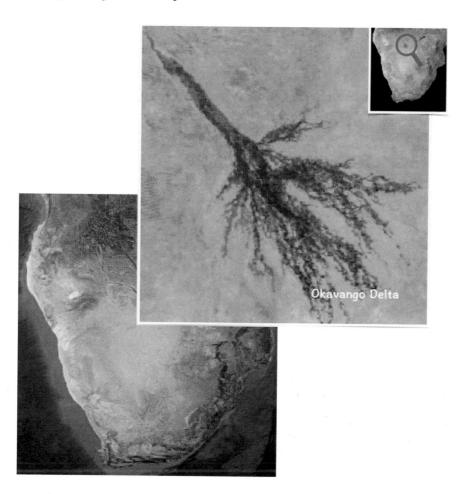

- **The Root of Life:** Located at Grandma Mt. Eve's temple is the center of Kalahari Desert, where the image of a giant tree root can be found. It is the Okavango Delta, one of Africa's greatest concentrations of wildlife diversity. Some researchers believe that areas like the Okavango Delta, with their rich biodiversity and stable water sources, might resemble the environments where early humans evolved.

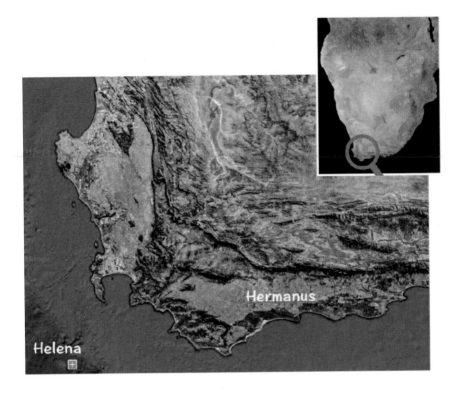

Helena

Hermanus

- **The Sphinx & Her-man-us:** Cape Peninsular of South Africa, which forms the jaw of Grandma Mt.Eve, Looks like a Sea Lion laying at the southern tip of Africa. It reveals a beautiful face, the archetype of the Sphinx. Also note that there is a town named "Her-man-us" and the bay surrounding it is named "Helena", same as the name of a saint who is the discover of the cross in Christian religion.

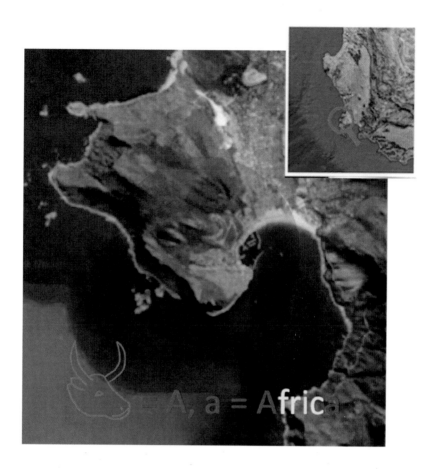

- **The Cape of Good Hope:** If you enlarge the jaw of the Sphinx on the map, you'll notice that the southern tip of Africa resembles the vivid head of a cow. This is the Cape of Good Hope. Here, we find the deep roots of the first alphabet and the first vowel, "A, a," whose Egyptian hieroglyph is a cow's head. This observation uncovers the reason why the names of our ancestral home continents—Africa, Asia, Australia, and America—all start and end with the letter "A, a." And same of the names of first four generations of goddess in Greek Mythology: Gaia, Rhea, Hera, and Athena.

In many myths and religions, such as Hinduism, the cow is revered as a sacred animal symbolizing the virtual of motherhood. In ancient Egyptian religion, the cow was associated with Hathor, the goddess of motherhood, love, and joy. Hathor was often depicted as a cow or with cow horns and ears. In the Chinese Zodiac, the cow is the first female (Yin) featured animal and the ancestor of Yan-Di (炎帝) has also an image of a cow-head. Cow is one of the first domesticated animal that still the main source of crucial nutrients human life depending on.

All these coincidences align with scientific findings that suggest South Africa is our motherland, the cradle of humanity, the deep female root of life on Earth.

3. The Fatherland of Eastern Africa

- **The Grandpa Y. Adam :** In contrast to the image of Eve in South Africa looking southwest, the image of eastern and central Africa forms a male head with the tip of his nose pointing northeast. I named him Grandpa Y. Adam, representing the far Y-chromosomal ancestor from whom all men share a common patrilineal heritage.

- **The Y-Gene Print :** Similar to the mark on Grandma Mt. Eve's temple, there is a significant mark on Grandpa Y. Adam's cheek, indicating the patriarchal origin of life. This mark is the Great Rift Valley, which forms a giant Y shape around Lake Victoria, the symbol of male gene. Interestingly, the shape of Lake Victoria resembles the portrait of Queen Victoria found on British coins. Additionally, one of the seven lakes surrounding Lake Victoria at the northernmost end is named Lake Albert, the same name as Queen Victoria's prince. The best-selected royal family gene in human history has much deeper roots than we are aware of.

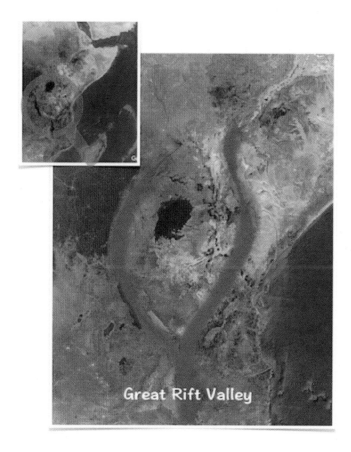

Great Rift Valley

- **The Ego of Man**. While the jaw of Grandma Mt. Eve at the southern tip of South Africa features the sacred cow head, symbolizing female nature, the eastern tip of Africa reveals the head of a dog or wolf. This symbolizes the hidden ego of male nature in humanity, suggesting that the eastern tip of Africa was the homeland of our paternal lineage. In the Chinese Zodiac, the cow is the first female animal, while the dog is the final male animal. The cow, a major source of survival nutrients, contrasts with the dog, humanity's most loyal companion in modern life. Notably, the word "dog" is the reversal of "god."

The Eastern Tip of Africa

All these seemingly unrelated coincidences intricately interconnect in a consistent common pattern, following symmetric Yin-Yang principles and beautiful logic. This reflects the fundamental nature of collective unconscious archetypes.

7.2 The Titans Out of Africa

After discovering the archetypes of our ancestors from Africa, I soon identified many vivid skeletons of Titans and Titanesses on Google Earth. Here are some examples:

1. The Titans

- **Prince of the Iberian Kingdom:** The Iberian Peninsula, shaped like the head of a young man, is formed by Spain and Portugal. I named it Prince Simba because his nose points towards the nose of the Lion King of Africa, as if receiving lessons from his father.

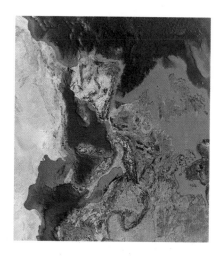

  He represents the head of Western Europe, analogous to a giant dinosaur, with Italy as its left arm and the fragmented British Isles as its right arm. This image provides insight into why Spain, despite its small size, became a pioneer of ocean navigation and a leading colonizer. Geographically, Spain's position on the Iberian Peninsula offers access to both the Atlantic Ocean and the Mediterranean Sea. Symbolically, Prince Simba's nose almost connects with that of the Lion King of Africa, suggesting an inherited mission from the God Father. As Carl Jung said, "Until you make the unconscious conscious, it will rule your life and you will call it Fate." This applies not only to the fate of individuals but also to the destiny of a nation.

- **The Father of the Sea People**: Situated in the middle of the Mediterranean Sea, below the Italian Peninsula, are the islands of Corsica and Sardinia. The flag of Sardinia features four black heads around a red cross, indicating this as the sacred fatherland of Mediterranean Sea People. In fact, Corsica and Sardinia are significant as the origin of the cross-flag in ancient history that date back to pre-Roman and Roman times. During these periods, the cross symbol was used in various contexts, including religious and cultural practices. The cross-flag was adopted by the Roman Empire and many subsequent European nations. The pareidolia view of these two islands from Google Earth appears like an ancient old man—or the skeleton of an ape—echoing the deep meaning of their flags symbolizing the original heads of the Mediterranean Sea People. Note once again the coincidence here, that the name of Corsica and Sardinia both inherit the same tail letter "a", the sacred cow head, from their common mother goddess Gaia. Next to the body of this ape, lies the beautiful body of Italy, looking like the giant body of a mermaid floating at the Mediterranean Sea.

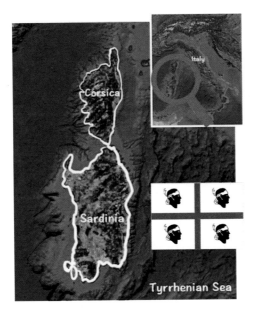

- **The Redeemers of South America**: Brazil and Argentina, as prominent pillars of the continent, resemble two colossal ape heads emerging from the Atlantic Ocean. Similar to the temple of Eve's head of South Africa, it's interesting to note that the Amazon River Estuary is located at the position of the "eye" on the head of Brazil. It echos the sense that the original meaning of the letter "O" for ocean is an eye. Also, the word "river" starts and ends with a human head, revealing the deep linkage of the Amazon River with these two giant heads of the American continents.

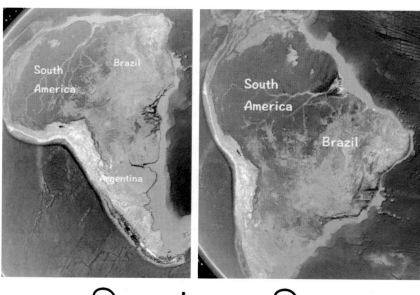

- **The Father of Southeast Asia**: Zooming in on Southeast Asia, you will find this primitive wonderland with an upright man pulling a bear in front of him and chased by a giant turtle. This is where the Coral Triangle is located, between the Pacific and Indian Oceans, recognized as a global hotspot for marine biodiversity, containing 76% of all known coral species in the world. As revealed by the vivid giant man figure of the islands, this region is quite likely one of the earliest origins of ancestral Asian fatherlands on Earth.

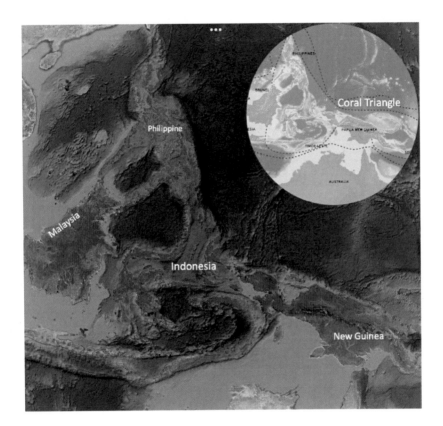

2. The Titanesses

- **The Fleeing Nymph of Middle East.** Situated below and between Simba and Lion King is the cross-land of Middle East. It is a diverse and ancient region that spans the continents of Africa, Asia, and Europe. Its geographical shape resembles a stretched nymph, symbolizing the perpetual conflicts that have plagued this sacred motherland.

- **The Enduring Spirit of Hope**. By zooming in on the image of the Dead Sea located near the left shoulder of the nymph of Middle East, a captivating scene unfolds at the sea's bottom. A stunning woman is seen alongside a giant green turtle, both gazing upward towards the land of Jerusalem. As the saying goes, "In the Middle East, history is not something you read about in books. Here, you can breathe it, touch it, and feel it with every step you take." This image reveals the profound connection between the region's rich history and the enduring spirit of hope from the "dead" sea.

- **The Mother Armenia.** Located at the right shoulder of the Nymph of Middle East is the motherland of Armenia, a small, landlocked Christian nation surrounded by mostly non-Christian neighbors. The contour of its map shows a shape of a beautiful woman's head. This explains anything about Armenia same as the iconic statue of The Mother Armenia in the capital city of Yerevan. It symbolizes peace through strength and represents the prominent female figures in Armenian history of endurance and survival. The name of Armenia, once again as many names of goddess, inherits the common origin of "A,a" from her mother-line ancestral genes of Africa.

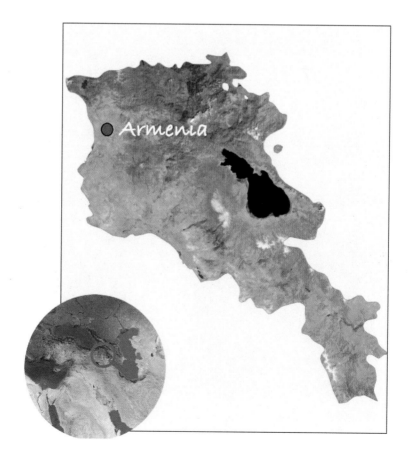

- **The Mommy Mummy of Madagascar.** Floating Below and next to the heads of Adam and Eve, is the Island of Madagascar which resembles a mummy of a female body. The seal of Madagascar includes this sacred body in the center of the sun and above the head of cow. All these indicate that this land is a home of sacred motherland carrying the root of motherliness genes from the holy cow.

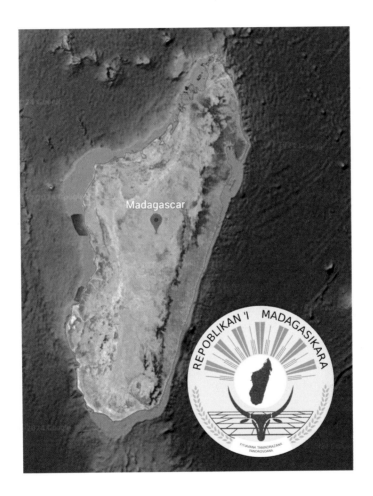

- **The Mother of India.** Zooming into the southern tip of India, you will discover a captivating image of a graceful woman's head. I named it The Mother of India. It is intriguing to observe that this location lies northeast of a straight line that connects Grandma Mt. Eve and Mommy-Mummy Madagascar. Here we found the deep roots of the female features that dominates Indian culture and history of harmony and peace. Once again, the name of India also inherits the tail-letter of "a", the head of holy cow as generally worshiped in Indian tradition.

- **The Mermaid of Italy**. This image may be the only one in this book that is not unfamiliar to most people. It showcases the captivating beauty of a renowned Italian landmark, reminiscent of the Danish fairy tale "The Little Mermaid" and represents the historical splendor of this romantic motherland.

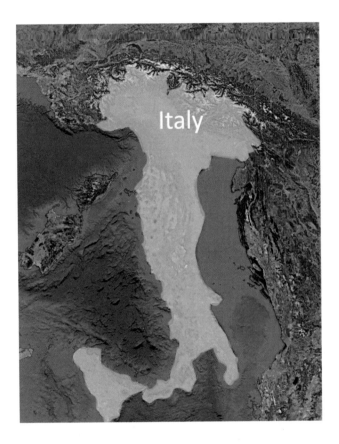

- **The Mermaid of Mexico.** Zooming in the Mexican coastline around the California Bay, you will find an upright mermaid laying along the shoreline. Her head is engraved at upper-left corner and her tail at the bottom-right connection to Costa Rica. This should be the archetype that shapes the mystery of Mexican culture and the tradition of worshiping the beauties of the ghosts.

7.3 The God's Footprints

1.Footprints of Cape Verde

Zooming in on the western coastline of West Africa, I saw the western face of Lion King Africa facing the west. In front of his eyes, lies the coral reef archipelago, the Cape Verde Islands. When further zooming into satellite view of Cape Verde Islands, it looks a giant foot print of a Loin. Coincidentally, the Chinese name of Cape Verde, 佛得角 (Fodejiao), sounds the same as "佛的脚-The Foot of Buddha".

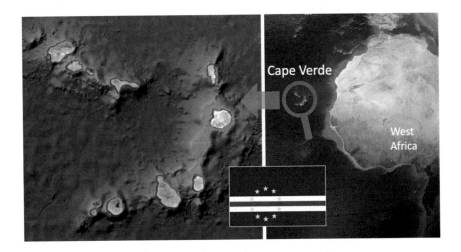

Cape Verde is famous for being the first stop of Darwin's Beagle voyage in 1831, marking the first time that humans took interest in atolls, and was the inspiration for Darwin's theory of atoll formation. The marine environment, where coral reefs thrive, is believed to be where life first originated. Study of coral reefs and their ecosystems can provide valuable information about the evolutionary and environmental contexts in which life on Earth developed. The flag of the Cape Verde Islands contains a red "blood line" streaking across the blue Atlantic Ocean with ten yellow stars forming a perfect circle, symbolizing a perfect start and end of life. The flag design revealed the significance of these islands related to life origin.

Several islands in the Cape Verde are named after the saints of the Bible. When I enlarged the satellite image of each island, I was surprised to find that the outline of the islands' coasts not only contain serene images of figures, but they also look like the saints their names imply. For Example:

2. Saint Peter and Saint Mary:

Sal Island, located at the northeast of Cape Verde, is a popular tourist destination. The name "Sal" originates from the Portuguese word for "Salvador" or "Savior". The unique topography of Sal Island resembles a totem, featuring stacked faces. Notably, a man and a woman are highlighted in red and green circles. Coincidentally, a village in the northeast called Pedra de Lune, which is equivalent to Saint Peter. Furthermore, a city in the southern region is named Santa Maria, same as Saint Mary in English. The pattern of female from lower south and male from upper north is quite common among places of life origin.

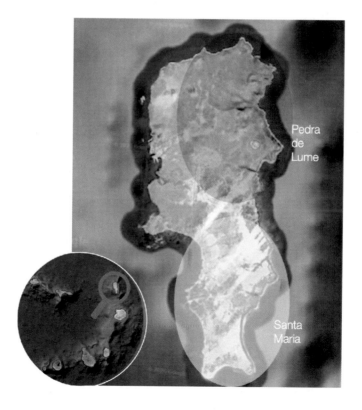

3. The Archetypes of Greek Gods

Greek mythology is renowned for its rich tapestry of stories featuring gods, heroes, and mortals. Zeus, the king of the gods, is symbolized by his powerful lightning bolt. An interesting coincidence lies in his name: the initial letter "Z," resembling the shape of lightning, originally meant "weapon" in hieroglyphs. Meanwhile, the tail letter "us" as a muscular suffix and the same of pronoun "us", represents the male nature of Zeus and the God of all of us.

Zeus was born on the southernmost island of Crete. The name "Crete" intriguingly resembles the word "create." Both share the initial letter "C," a primitive symbol of creation and civilization, and end with the letter "e," an archetype of humanity.

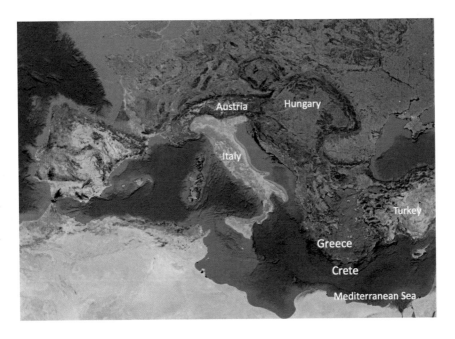

When I browse google earth images around Mediterranean Sea, I found this stunning picture of a giant man standing above the Crete Island, reaching his arm around the body of Mermaid Italy. It is like the archetype of Zeus with Greece being his right leg and Crete Island his right foot.

When I take a closer look at the Greek Islands, it's no surprise to find many islands named after and resembling figures from Greek mythology. Here are a few examples:

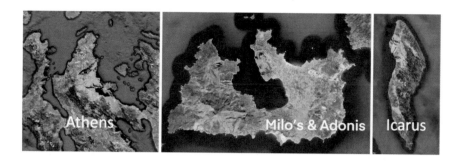

The most fascinating coincidence is the discovery that the influence of Greek gods seems to extend all the way to the northeastern tip of the European continent, marking a strategic "milestone" at the Bering Strait.

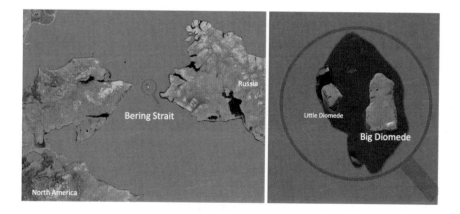

The image of the two sides of the Bering Strait resembles two giant beasts negotiating the ownership of the Diomede Islands. The submerged base of the islands forms a shadow resembling a human or ape head, while the two rocks of the Diomedes themselves appear like realistic heads.

Big Diomede, in particular, stands out like a statue of a saint. It's interesting to note that the name "Diomede" originates from a prominent character in Greek mythology, Diomedes. He is renowned as one of the greatest

Greek heroes of the Trojan War and a central figure in Homer's epic, the Iliad. Diomedes, the king of Argos, was a respected leader among the Greek forces, second only to Achilles. Known for his combat prowess, strategic acumen, and daring deeds, he remains a legendary figure in Greek epic poetry and myth.

The two mythical rocks of Diomedes symbolize the root of separation and the long Cold War between the two giant continents, the North America and Russia, intertwining mythology and the reality of our world.

4. The Archetypes of California Saints

I discovered from Google Earth three small islands in the California Bay that happen to bear the names of the three major cities of California: Isla Angel, Isla San Jose, and Isla San Francisco.

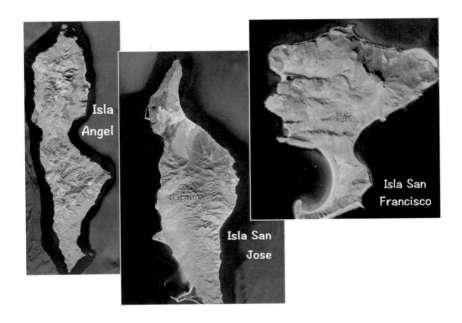

I was excited to find satellite images of each island resembling the character of the respective cities, each reflecting key features of their regional "temperament" or culture: a young lady for Los Angeles, a cool guy for San

Jose, and the dignified old lady for San Francisco. These "saints," as indicated in their names "Los-" or "San-", should be the ancestors of California people characterized by the archetypes with unique formations of these sacred islands.

7.4 The Shadows of Poseidon

1. The Superior Man:

Not only do many islands on Earth resemble the statues or skeletons of Titans, but numerous lakes also appear like the shadows of blue giants. The best example is North America's Great Lakes, which form a striking portrait of a superman, with Lake Superior as his head. Remarkably, the border between the U.S. and Canada divides this figure into two perfect halves across the middle of his body.

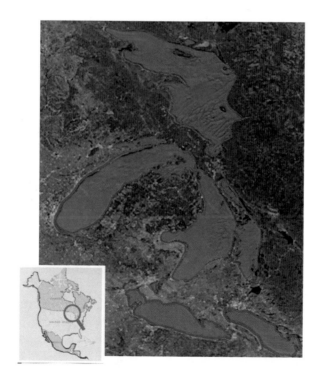

Imagine that, before the continents formed, the skeleton of a giant Titan sank into the ocean bed, creating a reservoir in his shape. As the ocean bed shifted and rose to become land, it formed the Great Lakes. This idea makes it unsurprising to find many other pareidolia lakes that reveal the endless cyclical patterns of life.

2. The Unchained Melody

The Ounianga Lakes, located in the Sahara Desert in northeastern Chad, are remnants of a much larger ancient lake system that existed during the Holocene period when the Sahara was a wetter region. The Ounianga Basin contains two groups of lakes: Kebir and Serir. Lake Yoa, the largest and most famous of the four lakes in the Kebir group, resembles the shape of a beautiful woman's head. The Serir group consists of 14 lakes that look like the lower bodies of men. Together, they evoke the touching theme of "The Ghost."

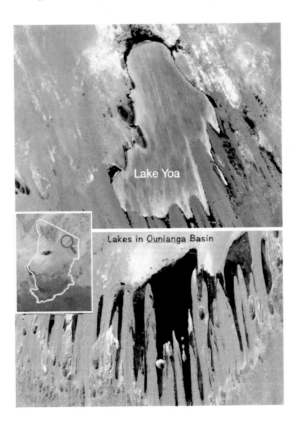

Lake Yoa

Lakes in Ounianga Basin

Interestingly, the names Serir and Kebir share the common suffix "ir," symbolizing a human arm and head, indicating a connection between these ancient lakes and the deep roots of human.

The Ounianga Lakes are an extraordinary example of resilience in the harsh desert, offering insights into past climatic conditions and the ongoing processes that sustain these unique ecosystems in the heart of the Sahara. They are of great interest to scientists studying climate change, hydrology, and desertification. From my perspective, they exemplify the unbroken connections between the beginnings and ends of life on Earth and so become the collect unconscious target of interest and protection as the important UNESCO world heritage site.

3. The Ape Fetus of Mediterranean Sea

I would like to conclude this chapter with a deep blue image of the Mediterranean Sea. Surrounded by Africa, Western Europe, and the Middle East, the Mediterranean Sea resembles an ape fetus. The Nile River acts as an umbilical cord, connecting the Mediterranean to its mother's water source, Lake Victoria. This imagery ties together the story of this book, beginning with the letter "e"—the human figure in its Egyptian origin—and, in its modern form, still retaining the circular shape of a fetus.

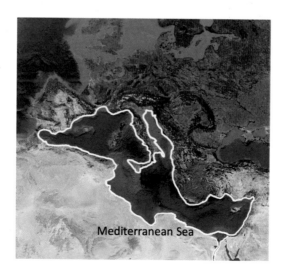
Mediterranean Sea

This giant "ape" fetus lies between the Lion King and Simba, linking the Greek god Zeus and the Roman Empire. In its brain, we find the islands of Corsica and Sardinia, home to the sacred Cross flag. Nowadays, people cruising on the Mediterranean Sea are often astonished by its clear, crystal blue water, unaware of a deeper truth: it reflects the Earth's connection with heaven in this sacred water where the roots of humanity and the souls of spirituality converge.

CHAPTER 8

THE UNCONSCIOUS MAP

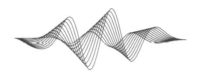

Incredibly, the topographic outlines of most borders, whether as large as a country or as small as a city, rarely feature straight lines. Instead, they follow curved, jagged contours that often resemble shapes such as animals or humans. These shapes frequently align with local legends or myths. Following the pattern of archetypes, regions closer to the origin of life often exhibit more explicit coincidences. For example, the topographic map of Shaanxi Province in China resembles the figure of an emperor (facing the southwest) or the Terracotta warriors buried in Xi'an. Xi'an, located in the hinterland of Shaanxi, was the first imperial capital of a unified China, established by Emperor Qin Shi Huang, who was also buried there.

8.1 The Sheep of China

Just as the African continent resembles a giant lion, the Lion King, the Eurasian super continent looks like a giant cow running over the globe toward east, with the northeastern tip of Russia as the head and the Middle East as the tail.

In the hinterland of this giant cow lies China, whose map resembles a giant sheep, with Northeast China forming the head facing east. The Mandarin name for China is "中国 (Zhōngguó)," meaning "middle kingdom," with "Zhōng (中)" meaning center, implying that China is the country at the center. The word for sheep in Chinese is "羊 (yáng)," which has many homophones such as "阳 (sun)," "洋 (ocean)," "氧 (oxygen)," and "养 (raise)," all crucial words related to life.

Interestingly, the English word "sheep" contains the head-word "she," and at the center of "sheep" is a couple of "ee," being the human archetypes. Notably, the words "shape" and "sheep" have similar spellings and sounds. Inside the word "shape," there is the tail-word "ape," combining the tail letter of "human" and the head letter of "cow." These seemingly unrelated coincidences are not far-fetched; They are like the intertwined roots in a forest of words, revealing deep, organic connections of life. You will not notice these pervasive coincidences until you bring your unconscious mind to consciousness.

In the Chinese Zodiac, the sheep is the fourth female animal sign, known for its representation of kindness, wisdom, and harmonious nature. This animal closely represents the general temperament of the Chinese people, who value "善良 (kindness)" and prefer living harmoniously in social groups. Notably, the word "善 (kind)" contains the character "羊 (sheep)" at the top, similar to "洋 (ocean)," "氧 (oxygen)," "养 (raise)," and "恙 (illness)." The Chinese believe they are descendants of Emperor Yan and Huang. Emperor Yan is often depicted with a human body and a cow's head, and the character for his surname, Jiang (姜), is composed of the sheep character on top above the character "女 (woman)."

These coincidences suggest that the map's shape resembling a sheep has unconsciously influenced the core features and values of the Chinese people and culture highlighting the nurturing nature of their motherland, the Middle Kingdom on Earth. You might wonder why the Chinese identify themselves as dragons rather than sheep. This can be best explained by the concept of Yin-Yang and the following coincidence of map shapes. Note that the word Yang (male) shares the same pronunciation as Yang for sheep. Within the motherland of the female sheep, a male dragon can be found at the center of China on Google Maps embraced by the emperor -the shape of Shaanxi's map as shown previously.

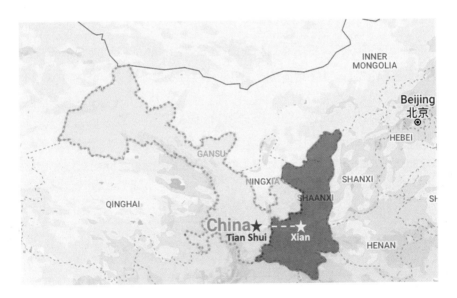

The significance of this map coincidence is that, to the right of the mark of "China" on google map, lies a historic city named "天水 (Tianshui)," literally meaning "water from heaven." This city is the birthplace of the Chinese paternal ancestor Fuxi. More significantly, both the legendary Emperor Huang Di and the first emperor to unify China, Qin Shi Huang, were born in Xi'an, which is aligned laterally with Fuxi's birthplace toward the east.

The coincidence that the "China" label on Google Maps is collocated with Tianshui City indicates this as the center of China's territory, the heart of the sheep. It explains how this Yang (male) dragon was born from the female sheep of China's landscape, just as the words "Female," "Woman," and "She" all contain the male counterpart within them. Furthermore, the name "China" carries the tail letter "a" from the sacred cow, and the capital letter "C" symbolizes creation, change, and civilization, and also the origin of letter "G" for God, Go, and Grow.

Let's delve into the deep roots of Yin-Yang philosophy, one of the most profound aspects of Chinese thought. Yin and Yang represent opposite sides of a duality. Generally, Yang is associated with the upper, vertical, and uplifting aspects, while Yin corresponds to the lower, horizontal, and recessive aspects. These principles can be consistently observed in the shapes of maps.

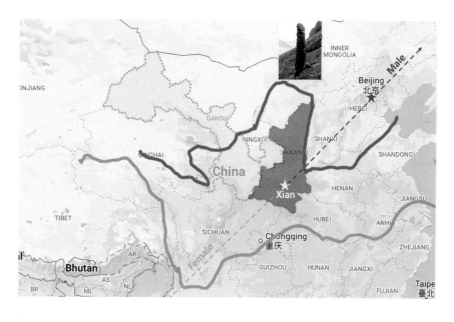

China is home to two significant rivers: the Yellow River in the north and the Yangtze River in the south. These rivers embody the opposing characteristics of Yin and Yang. The Yellow River, extending northward with a pronounced uplift toward the northeast, exhibits a typical Yang or male nature. In contrast, the Yangtze River flows southward with a notable downturn toward the southwest, displaying a typical Yin or female nature.

Regions north of the Yellow River are considered northern China, and those south of the Yangtze are deemed southern China. Traditionally, Chinese people from the north and the south are referred to as "北方人" (northern people) and "南方人" (southern people), reflecting distinct cultural differences aligned with masculine and feminine characteristics. Despite a long history of intermingling among various regions, the cultural differences between northern and southern China still remain quite obvious.

The Yellow River flows through Northeast China, a region whose inhabitants are often described as having strongly masculine temperaments. This includes the three northeast provinces and Inner Mongolia. Conversely, the Yangtze River flows toward the southwest, where locals are thought to possess more feminine characteristics, such as those in Sichuan and Yunnan Provinces.

An example of the extreme male region in the northeast is the history of the Mongol Empire founded by Genghis Khan, which included both Inner Mongolia and Mongolia. This history has deeply shaped the male-dominated culture in this region. In addition, an interesting geographical feature in Inner Mongolia is a gigantic rock pillar standing majestically near the highest point (extreme Yang) of the Yellow River. This pillar is nearly 30 meters tall and requires over a dozen people to encircle it. Predominantly reddish-brown in color, it is named "人根峰" (Ren Gen Peak), meaning "the sacred root of humanity." This pillar has inspired countless poets and scholars to compose verses about it throughout history and has become a worship site for people praying for fertility and venerating masculine power.

Opposite to the northeast, at the lowest recession (extreme Yin) of the Yangtze River lies the province of Yunnan, the most feminine region, home to China's only remaining matriarchal society, known as the "kingdom of daughters." Here, the Mosuo people maintain a matrilineal clan system and the custom of "walking marriages."

Another example of the male-dominated direction along the northeast is the location of capitals in Chinese history. Cities like Xian, Luoyang (He Nan), and Beijing are all along the line toward the Northeast. The last emperor in China history, the last emperor of the Qing Dynasty, Pu Yi, died in Harbin at the far end of Northeast China. Conversely, if you extend the line southwest beyond China, you will find more female-dominated countries in Asia, such as Myanmar and India. In fact, if you look back at the geography of Africa as presented in Chapter 7, you will find the same pattern: the root of the motherland (Eve) at the southwestern tip and the root of the fatherland (Adam) at the northeastern tip.

8.2 The White Horse of Russia

Above the "sheep" of China on the map of Eurasia lies its neighbor, Russia. As the largest country in the world, spanning Eastern Europe and northern Asia, Russia is a significant geopolitical player. The map of Russia resembles a giant leaping horse over Central Asia. Coincidentally, the national emblem of Russia features a white horse at its core. In Chinese Zodiac, the sheep symbolizes Yin or female nature, while the horse represents Yang or male nature. Just as the sheep embodies the core values of kindness and social harmony in Chinese culture, the horse represents Russia's strength, balanced power, and endurance.

Russia has been a central force in global history, from the establishment of Kievan Rus' in the 9th century to its major role in both World Wars and the Cold War. Its rich cultural heritage in literature, music, and the arts, along with achievements in science and space exploration, have cemented its place in human progress. Historically, China has referred to Russia as "the big brother."

Interestingly, when considering the western border nations of the former Soviet Union, such as Belarus, Ukraine, and Georgia, as highlighted in light green color in above figure, along with countries once part of the Russian Empire, like Finland and Poland, the figure of the giant horse becomes more perfectly defined.

Russia is divided into two major parts: European Russia in Europe and Siberia in Asia. The Ural Mountains and the Ural River delineate this division, bisecting the Eurasian supercontinent. European Russia, though smaller in area, is the most densely populated region and includes all three federal cities of Russia, such as Moscow and Saint Petersburg. It accounts for about 75% of Russia's total population, of which about 90% are Caucasian. Thus, although much of Russia's landmass lies in Asia, its population and cultural identity are predominantly European. So I name the horse of Russian map the "White Horse." In both Western and Asian cultures, the white horse symbolizes purity, nobility, and victory. In Western culture, Saint George, a prominent figure in Christian folklore, is depicted riding a white horse and is known for slaying a dragon to rescue a princess, symbolizing bravery, faith, and triumph over evil. This image at the core of Russia's national emblem reflects the fundamental "white" nature of Russia.

At the far foot of the giant White Horse of Russia, or the horse shoe, are the three Caucasus countries: Georgia, Armenia, and Azerbaijan. They were part of the Soviet Union and became independent in 1991 after its collapse. Georgia, named after Saint George, also features the image of Saint George on a white horse at the center of its emblem.

Georgia

Russia

A comparison between the national emblems of Georgia and Russia yields interesting insights. The Saint George figure on Georgia's emblem faces west and conquers a white dragon, while the Russian one faces east and conquers a black dragon. This suggests that the Georgian Saint George is an even "purer" white version. In Chinese, there is a homophonic coincidence between the words "远足" (far foot) and "元祖" (far ancestor), implying that Georgia, being at the far foot of the giant horse, could be the far ancestor of Russia's White Horse.

Historically, Johann Friedrich Blumenbach, an 18th-century German anthropologist known as the "founder of racial classifications," considered the people of the Caucasus region, particularly Georgians, to be exemplary of the Caucasian race due to their harmonious features. The Georgians are one of the oldest ethnic groups in the Caucasus, with a culture dating back to the Bronze Age. Relics discovered there trace back to the Paleolithic era, about 1.8 million years ago. Most Georgians today have Georgian ethnicity, comprising about 70% of the population. The Georgian language, part of the Caucasian language family, has an original alphabet used since the 3rd century BC.

Georgians traditionally claim that they are descent from Japheth, son of Noah, who is considered an ancestor of both Asians and Europeans. The flag of Georgia, with a red cross on a white background and four smaller red crosses, closely resembles the flag of Sardinia, highlighting deep connections between Georgians and European Caucasians.

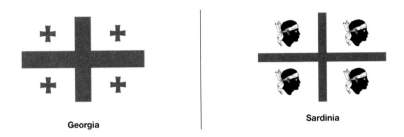

Georgia   **Sardinia**

Although modern science does not support all these historical and cultural connections, they reflect the collective unconscious in line with the prevalent views of the 18th century. These connections exemplify how imagination can bridge gaps in limited knowledge.

8.3 The Human Seeds from Centers

The word "seed" contains a pair of human archetype "ee" at its center, with the tail-letter "d"-a fish resembling animal root. Additionally, the Chinese word "种" for seed sounds the same as "中" for center. Notably, the word "center" ends with the letter "r," representing a human head, while the word "earth" has the letter "r" at its core center. These coincidences suggest a broader truth: humans are the central seeds of life. This is evident from our origins in a middle stage of life on Earth and the fact that most populations live in central locations of continents. In this section, I will share some coincidences I've found among maps, which often feature shapes resembling a human head located at the center of regions.

1. Chad in North-Central Africa

The map of Central Africa forms an upright figure of a man, with Chad as the head on the northern end. It stands out to the north of Grandma Mt. Eve (South Africa) and west of Grandpa Y. Adam (East Africa).

A landlocked country in north-central Africa, Chad is known for its diverse geography, including the Sahara Desert in the north, the arid Sahelian belt in the center, and the fertile Sudanian Savanna zone in the south. Chad is home to over 200 ethnic and linguistic groups, making it one of the most culturally diverse countries in Africa. Its strategic location made Chad a crucial hub for trans-Saharan trade routes, facilitating the exchange of goods and cultures between North Africa, West Africa, and the Nile Valley. Notable archaeological discoveries in Chad, such as the 7-million-year-old Toumai fossil, provide crucial insights into early human evolution, making Chad a significant location in the study of human origins.

2. Armenia in the South-Central Caucasus

Located in the South Caucasus region of Eurasia, Armenia is a landlocked country bordered by Turkey to the west, Georgia to the north, Azerbaijan to the east, and Iran to the south. Its topography features the silhouette of a woman's head, similar to the head of Chad in Africa.

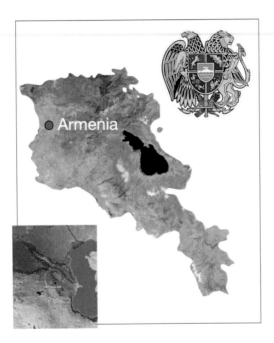

Like Africa, the name Armenia starts and ends with "A,a" symbolizing a cow's head, which represents the region's nature as a motherland. The woman's head in Armenia's map resembles the head of Eve of South Africa, suggesting a lineage from the ancestral Eve of South Africa.

Armenia boasts one of the world's oldest civilizations, with a history dating back to around 860 BC with the Kingdom of Urartu. Its historical and cultural legacy, particularly its early adoption of Christianity and its tragic experiences in the 20th century, have left a lasting mark on human history.

Armenia's national emblem reflects its central, balanced nature, a key aspect of humanity. It features four symbols in the middle layer: a double-headed eagle in the northeast, similar to Russia's emblem; lions in the northwest and southeast, akin to Georgia's emblem; and a pair of birds in the southwest, representing ancient Armenia. At the core is Mount Ararat rising from white ocean waves. According to Genesis, Noah's Ark came to rest on Mount Ararat. This mountain has been a spiritual symbol for Armenians since ancient times, who believe they were among the first to survive the great flood.

3. Iraq in the Middle East

The Middle East is not only the birthplace of the three major monotheistic religions but also the cradle of many ancient civilizations. The world's oldest civilization, known as the Sumerians or Mesopotamian civilization, emerged in this region. Here, humans first learned to domesticate animals, cultivate grains, and develop written record-keeping. The Euphrates and Tigris rivers were the lifeblood of this early civilization, originating in the northernmost reaches of modern-day Turkey and merging in present-day Iraq before flowing into the Persian Gulf. Abraham, the common ancestor of the Islamic, Jewish, and Christian faiths, was born in Ur, located where these rivers converge.

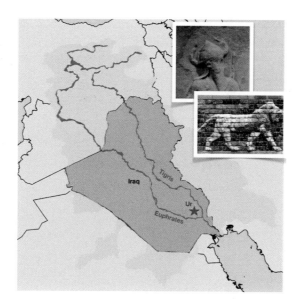

Situated in the middle of the Mesopotamian valley, the map of Iraq resembles a giant human head, which also looks like a lion's head, facing the east. This area has been inhabited for over 200,000 years and contains more ruins of past civilizations than any other place on earth. While Armenia may be seen as the daughter of the South African Eve, Iraq represents the son of the African Lion King.

An interesting coincidence is that the basins of the Euphrates and Tigris rivers form the silhouette of a cow, with the two rivers themselves tracing the shape of an antelope inside the cow. This mirrors the pattern seen in Eurasia, where the continent forms the shape of a giant cow with China resembling a sheep within it. The Mesopotamian civilization was pivotal in developing animal husbandry and agriculture. According to Sumerian legends, prosperity arrives when the gods "make the sheep bear lambs and create a bumper harvest of grains." Ancient Sumerian murals depict idols wearing bull-horned hats, and their tradition of using sheep to honor the gods has endured through the ages. The sacred cow and sheep's historical significance serves as geographical representations of collective unconscious archetypes at the cradle of civilization.

4. Belarus in Central East Europe

The phenomenon of "human head at the center" appears once again in the topography of Belarus. Situated in the heart of Eastern Europe, Belarus's landscape resembles the portrait of a large-nosed human head facing east.

The ending "rus" in Belarus is the same as the beginning "Rus" in Russia. "Rus" is the root of the word used by the East Slavs to refer to the Nordic people and is the same prefix found in Roslagen, the northern coast of Sweden. The Rus originated from the Vikings on the east coast of Sweden in the 8th century, hence the term Viking Rus. From the 13th to the 14th century, Western Europeans referred to the Christian Slavs in the area around modern Belarus as the White Rus, and the Baltic pagans as the Black Rus. Today, Ukrainians are sometimes called Red Rus.

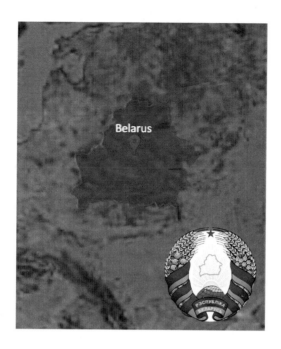

The "Rus" at the end of Belarus symbolizes the head of Russia, mirroring the geography where Belarus is located at the hip of the "horse" of Russia presented before, implying that Belarus is the root of the white Slavs in Russia. The name "Belarus" can be broken down as "Be+la+rus," meaning "It is the Rus." Interestingly, "Bel" sounds similar to the Chinese word "白" (bái), meaning white. Thus, the Chinese name for Belarus is "白俄罗斯" (Báiéluósī), which means "White Russia."

In Belarusian tradition, white is considered a holy color, and Belarusians often favor white clothing. From many perspectives, Belarus has demonstrated itself to be the pure white Slav ancestral seed of Eastern Europe.

The examples above are just a few of many that I discovered on world maps. Reflecting on these coincidences led me to find another meaningful word coincidence: the Mongolian word for river, the origin of life, is "hyyp" which follows a pattern similar to the word "seed." The first letter, "h," represents "sunlight," and the last letter, "p" (for penis or person), indicates human roots. The two "yy" sit in the center of hyyp (river). The letter "Y," a symbol of the human male gene, resembles the basic shape of a tree and the common initial form of various plants. Using fractal simulations of tree growth, I found that after four "generations" of self replication, the shape "Y" produces a large hexagonal ring-shaped body in the center with a small star at the top—symbolizing the "seed" and "fruit," much like the human head at the top end of human body.

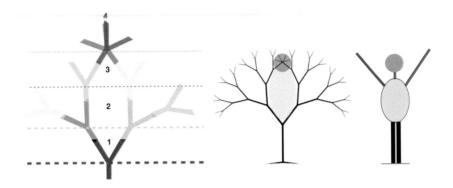

This explains the universal pattern of seeds and fruits appearing pre-dominantly at the center top because they receive the most sunlight and are the balanced result of diverse roots. When drawing the evolutionary tree of Chinese history from the common legend ancestor Huang Di, I discovered that Qin Shihuang, the first real emperor in history who unified China, is positioned right at the central top of the tree. Similarly, in my family tree spanning over 300 years, my father, the first to move from a rural village to the capital city and the first college graduate, also occupies the central top position of the whole family tree. Applying this pattern on a larger scale, it becomes evident that humans, with their balanced nature, occupy the central top position in the evolutionary tree of animals on Earth, leading to their outstanding power of dominance.

To conclude this chapter, I would like to share two examples from nature where I found vivid human heads at the tops of trees and a cat's head at the core center of a beautiful flower. These old trees can be found in many places in California, especially at the historic site of Lombard Street in San

Francisco. The flower is a type of white orchid that grows widely across the globe.

Curiosity, observation, and imagination are the most crucial instincts for uncovering the many secrets of nature in our daily lives. While science tells us that humans evolved from plants to animals, messengers of collective coincidences provide evidence of universal reversal patterns, suggesting that humans could also be the origin of all life, or even the whole universe in human perception. While religions ask us to believe that God created humans, there is compelling evidence that God could have been created by humans.

The word for "river," which is the cradle of life and the veins of Mother Earth, carries the human head "r" from beginning to end. The origin of its Chinese character reveals an even more profound picture: two humans turning around each other. In Pinyin, its pronunciation is "He" — the same spelling as "he" in English, which is also used to represent God in the Bible.

The power of ration and imagination has endowed me with the rational belief that a human being is a microcosm—a small universe. Individually, we are mortal, but collectively, we are immortal and eternal. In personal consciousness, we are finite, but in the collective unconscious, we transcend time and space. This interplay between science, faith, and imagination invites us to see ourselves as integral parts of an eternal, universal story, where every discovery, every coincidence, and every act of creation is a testament to our enduring place in the cosmos.

CHAPTER 9

MAKING UNCONSCIOUS MIND CONSCIOUS

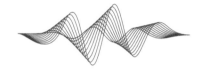

9.1 The Power of Focus

There are moments when I question whether all the discoveries I've made are mere illusions, invisible to ordinary minds. But, why do these coincidences persistently emerge, imbued with meaning for me?

Once, while taking a picture on a hiking trail, capturing distant lights casting a glow over a bush, a passing lady inquired about my focus and attraction. Showing her the photo, she exclaimed, "It's stunning! Thank you for revealing it to me; I would never have noticed." Indeed, without the focused lens of a camera, many scenes go unnoticed.

Another time, at a friend's mindfulness seminar, the teacher conducted an exercise demonstrating mindfulness through sound. She asked us to close our eyes as she struck a bell. The first strike yielded a short tinkling sound; with each subsequent strike, the ringing grew longer. The teacher explained that the bell was struck consistently the same each time—the difference lay in our attentive perception. By closing our eyes and fully concentrating on the sound, we blocked out surrounding noises and honed in on the final reverberations, normally obscured by background clamor.

Reflecting on this experience on my way home, I felt a surge of understanding. I now grasped why Buddhists close their eyes to meditate and why devout piety is integral to Christian prayer. It also shed light on my ability to discern unconscious patterns that others overlook. The key, I realized, lies in focused attention. When you concentrate on a phenomenon, you silence the background noise that typically muddles consciousness, unveiling signals from the deep layers of the collective unconscious.

However, making the unconscious mind conscious doesn't come easily, especially for those rooted in empirical thinking. Beyond focus, I've found other principles that have helped me comprehend these unique insights derived from the collective unconscious.

9.2 Normal Distribution and Extreme Effects

Those versed in statistical methods might find my attempts to derive universal laws from a few coincidences at odds with scientific principles. In my early days, I grappled with this question myself. A pivotal shift occurred a decade ago.

In 2010, an unexpected relationship presented me with new challenges and choices. Curious about its future, I consulted a colleague skilled in the "Yi Jing" for a fortune reading. Initially skeptical, I challenged him to redo the reading—wouldn't the outcome differ? He rejected and explained that the first reading holds sway, emphasizing that divination pertains only to significant events and pivotal life junctures. Though unconvinced at the time, I now marvel at how accurately his prediction unfolded in my life. The principles of divination and coincidence share similarities: not all occurrences equally exhibit certain patterns, but only key events align distinctly with overarching laws.

This insight hinges on understanding the "bell curve," which delineates normal distribution, and the "well curve," illustrating the impact of individual instances as depicted by the red and blue curves respectively in the figure below.

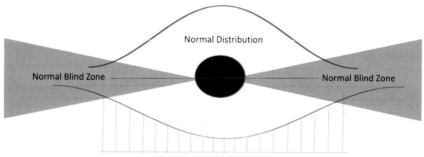

Well Curve of Individual Impact on the whole

The distribution of natural phenomena and attributes typically adheres to the normal distribution, often represented by the bell curve. For example, adult heights cluster around a central range between 1.5m and 1.8m, with fewer individuals below 1.4m or above 2m. We commonly regard samples within this middle range as "normal." When generalizing about phenomena, we gather a large number of samples to ensure statistical significance, filtering out outliers.

Yet, it's often those outliers at the extremes of the normal distribution that exert a disproportionate influence on the overall pattern, depicted by an inverse bell curve known as the "well curve." For instance, movements in the stock market are significantly impacted by trends in the largest companies, more so than by numerous mid-sized companies combined. Similarly, a company's performance is often most affected by its top and bottom 15% of employees, and history has been shaped by the actions of a select few key individuals in history.

This phenomenon explains why extreme cases can significantly alter the curve more than typical cases, and why divination is more accurate at pivotal moments. Most renowned fortune tellers focus on emperors and other highly influential figures not just due to their wealth, but because their fates align closely with the generalized rules governing broader outcomes. This parallels how a handful of major companies can predict market trends more effectively than extensive data sampling across the entire market.

Confucius encapsulated life's rhythms in his saying: "aspiring to learn at fifteen, independent at thirty, without doubt at forty, know thy destiny at fifty, do as you please at sixty..." Derived from personal insight, this pattern remains relevant as a general pattern of life even millennia later, because he is an extreme individual that is called "the man of a millennia."

Through the lens of the bell curve and well curve, we discern how profoundly impactful individuals conform to universal patterns and rules that underpin the collective unconscious. In linguistics, highly used keywords or "key letters" often follow predictable patterns, such as the prevalence of the letter "e" and the significance of words like "DOG & GOD" and "evolve."

Many examples in this book draw from extreme individual cases along the normal distribution, illuminating hidden, common rules of collective unconscious archetypes. I believe this mirrors how the ancient Chinese discovered the principles of yin-yang theory and the Yi Jing, distilling universal laws from direct observation of phenomena. These principles apply universally to life, transcending the need for extensive big data tools. However, if these coincidences garner widespread interest in the future and become the subject of analytical big data studies, more accurate rules and logic will emerge, revealing more meaningful patterns.

9.3 Yin-Yang Polarized View

Yin and Yang represent China's ancient philosophical cornerstone and the most refined abstraction of natural laws. Analogous to a binary code of "0" and "1," it subtly influences both our lives and the natural world. Originating over 2,000 years ago, Yin and Yang were conceived by our ancestors who relied solely on instinct and observation to interpret nature. They discerned that everything possesses dual, opposing aspects: male and female, heaven and earth, day and night, cold and heat, vertical and horizontal, up and down, and more. From the concept of Yin and Yang, many philosophical traditions emerged, including the Yi Jing, Daoism, and Traditional Chinese Medicine. The natural principles of Yin and Yang can be summarized in three key points:

1. Everything embodies two fundamental opposites: Yin and Yang.

2. These principles are unified yet opposing—Yang contains Yin, and Yin contains Yang.

3. They are relative, in constant flux, and mutually transformative. The peak of Yin transitions into Yang, and vice versa.

Yin-Yang provides a polarized perspective of the world. Initially defined simply as male (Yang) and female (Yin), everything was categorized into Yin or Yang pairs: the sun as Yang and the moon as Yin, fire as Yang and water as Yin. Assigning gendered attributes to genderless entities might seem arbitrary, yet these attributions surprisingly justify themselves.

Consider the application of Yin and Yang attributes to numbers. There appears to be no obvious reason why odd numbers should be Yang and even numbers Yin. This curiosity prompted me to explore how consistently nature adheres to these principles.

For example, female and male gene are distinguished by the symbols X and Y respectively, while letter X has two strokes (even-Yin), letter Y has three strokes (Odd-Yang). Another example of how the 12 animals of the Chinese zodiac are classified into two groups: 6 females and 6 males. The female animals such as pigs, cows, sheep, chickens all have an even number of toes (two & four), while the male animals such as tiger, monkeys, dinosaur and humans all have an odd number of toes (five). Intriguingly, the horse which lies in the middle of the 12 zodiac is known for its nature of a balanced yang animal. Horse's hoof is in a "0" shape (even), and if you look closely you will notice a triangular (3-odd) frame inside: "Yang inside of Yin" - the Tai-ji state.

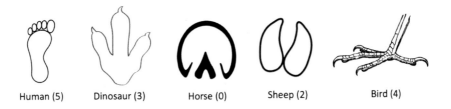

Human (5)   Dinosaur (3)   Horse (0)   Sheep (2)   Bird (4)

The Taiji diagram, also known as the "Supreme Ultimate" symbol in the West, vividly embodies the natural law of Yin and Yang: a unity comprising two opposing forces. It features a black fish marked by a white eye (dot), and a white fish with a black eye.

Once you grasp the principles of Yin and Yang, the chaotic world begins to take on orderliness. It's akin to looking through polarized lenses underwater, filtering out reflections and offering a clearer view of the submerged environment. Imagine donning Yin-Yang polarized glasses as you delve into the examples I presented in this book and you will see through the deep water the clear pictures of order out of chaos.

9.4 Awareness of Archetype and Instinct

The keys to unraveling the secrets of the collective unconscious lie in the dual concepts of instinct and archetype. These concepts often challenge our conventional understanding. That's why I frequently include quotes from

Carl Jung in my books. I've found through experience that grasping someone else's true meaning often requires repeated reading. Each time I revisit Jung's writings, I uncover new insights and deeper understanding of his words.

Jung discovered that many of his psychiatric patients hallucinated biblical stories even though those patients had never read the Bible. His archetype concept was inspired by the ancient bishop Irenaeus: "The creator of the world did not fashion these things directly from himself but copied them from archetypes outside himself." Jung concluded that man's unconsciousness contains remote archaic patterns and instincts inherited from the ancestors:

> "...so far as the collective unconscious contents are concerned we are dealing with archaic or—I would say—primordial types, that is, with universal images that have existed since the remotest times... The archetype is essentially an unconscious content that is altered by becoming conscious and by being perceived, and it takes its color from the individual consciousness in which it happens to appear."
>
> —CARL JUNG

Understanding the primal essence of archetypes, rooted in the ancient concept denoted by the prefix "Arche," I've discovered that the most direct path to uncovering the deep layers of the collective unconscious is through focusing on "primitive" forms that are least influenced by individual consciousness. Just as trees, despite their varied leaves and flowers, all originate from similar seeds, deep roots, and shoots, common forms, rules, and a coherent logic also emerge from the foundational roots of words and our human essence. When I search for significant coincidences among words—beyond the keywords mentioned earlier—I often discover them within the universal patterns found in the origins of words, such as the earliest Chinese characters derived from oracle bone inscriptions and ancient hieroglyphic alphabets. Similarly, more unconscious connections can be found in the pronunciation of words rather than their written structure, as the sound of words has deeper roots in spoken language. The same rules apply to pareidolia coincidences. It's easier to find them among most primitive regions that is closer to the origin of life, and looking for more significant examples in history of humanity.

"In all chaos, there is a universe and a secret order; among all phenomenas, there is a unified law...What we call complexity and miracles is not complicated and magical at all in nature, on the contrary, it is simple and common. We are used to project our own difficulties in understanding to things and to describe them as complex, but in fact, they are very simple and do not understand the difficulties we encounter intellectually."

–CARL JUNG

The path to enlightenment is paved with archetypes. Whenever we encounter recurring patterns of life, we are touching upon archetypes. Most examples in my book are either extreme or in the most original form. In the same way, you will find a lot pareidolia images with ease from rocks of the ancient geology sites, as well as from google map of more significant historical regions.

With these archetype hammers in hand and fit with polarized goggles, you are prepared to dive to the seabed and knock on the door of the collective unconscious. Through its frame lies an unprecedented new world waiting for us to explore. All you need is practice and practice until the deep world of collective unconscious floats into your conscious naturally.

ABOUT THE AUTHOR

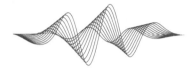

Helen Sevic, also known by her Chinese name Xuguang Yu, was born in Penglai, Shandong province. She enrolled at Tsinghua University in 1981, where she spent 11 years and earned her Ph.D. in mechanical engineering in 1992. Helen then spent 11 years at IBM in China and another decade at various leading global high-tech companies before immigrating to the United States in 2013.

From a young age, Helen has harbored a profound curiosity about life and nature. Her quest to understand humanity's origins and the possibility of past lives culminated in the creation of DOG & GOD. Her extensive education in Science and Engineering honed her logical thinking but instilled a skepticism toward accepting beliefs without understanding their reasons. Inspired by Carl Jung's concept of the collective unconscious and archetypes, she found a pathway to reconcile belief with understanding.

This journey has ignited a wealth of new ideas and discoveries in the realm of coincidences through observation and imagination, effectively bridging the gap between science and myth. Helen regards this book as her bold, unconventional thesis, the true passion of a lifelong pursuit. She sees it as a profound exploration into the depths of the collective unconscious, where countless mysteries await unraveling. By bringing unconscious thoughts to the surface, she envisions uncovering answers to many of humanity's enigmatic questions.